THE GHOSTS
OF
MAKARA

*Growing Up Down-Under In a
Lost World of Yesteryears*

Bernard Diederich

To order additional copies of this book, contact:
Xlibris Corporation
1-888-795-4274
www.Xlibris.com
Orders@Xlibris.com
15464-DIED

To Alberto:
A friend for life
with best wishes
for a better tomorrow
for our Nation.

un abrazo

Bernd.

11-19-03
Miami FL.

Also by Bernard Diederich

Papa Doc: The Truth About Haiti. With Al Burt.
Trujillo: Death of The Goat
Somoza: The Legacy of U.S. Involvement in Central America

Dedication

This memoir is dedicated to Mum and Dad, Stellamaris, Quita, Brian, Geoffrey and Patrick and all those others who were part of my extended family, but who are no longer with us. I owe so much to their love and guidance as well as to my non-ghost patient spouse, Ginette.

Natalie, Jean-Bernard and Phillippe, our beloved children, fell in love with New Zealand on their early childhood visits and often would ask, "Tell us what it was like growing up in Makara and New Zealand." And my grandson Alexandre Bernard who cannot wait to visit grandpa's homeland.

AUTHOR'S NOTE

A happy family is but an earlier heaven.

-Sir John Bowring (1792-1872, English statesman

If children are a gift of God, growing up in a large and contented family is a benediction of the saints. This book is a very personal memoir about such a family—my family. And these recollections are made all the more wistful by the time period and the setting in which my sisters and brothers and I, cosseted and disciplined by a solicitous Irish-New Zealand Mum and a hard working German-Irish-New Zealand Dad, grew into adolescence.

The time was the 1920s and 30s, a period encompassing the Great Depression and presaging World War II—truly the end of an era. The setting was a rocky, windswept, virtually unknown outcropping of New Zealand known as Makara Beach.

That was where I—or, more specifically, we Diederich offspring—played, fought, explored, learned about both our colonial roots and New Zealand's indigenous Maori culture, and huddled in our beds at night listened to the fearful howling winds, which childhood imagination transformed into the ghosts of Makara.

And it was from Makara and the nearby city of Wellington that I sailed away, as a sixteen-year-old cabin boy on the majestic four-masted barque PAMIR, its 34 sails billowing in the wind, to see the larger world. It was a great privileged to sail before the mast and experience the manner of travel that brought my ancestors to New Zealand in the nineteenth century.

Today, few can afford the luxury of a big family. Families have gotten smaller, for understandable, if often regrettable, reasons. Health costs and sending a child to college can devour a lifetime of saving. Both parents frequently must work, adding to the normal

stresses of the family environment. A typical modern child grows
up with television as a substitute Mum.

To me, it is truly heart-rending to realize that many a youngster today—bused in the morning to impersonal schools in distant neighborhoods, relegated in the afternoon to day-care centers—will never know what it is like to come home to a waiting
Mum, and join her and Dad and brothers and sisters at a conviv-
ial, TV-free dinner table.

As I note in my Epilogue, they are gone now—Mum and Dad;
my big sister Stellamaris who lived her adult life as a caring Sister
of Mercy nun and died of cancer in 1986; my sister Marquita
(Quita) with a wonderful family of six children in Australia who
died also of cancer a decade later; even that four-masted barque
that carried me away, itself sunk in a hurricane off the Azores in
1957 with eighty hands lost.

And even the ghosts of Makara, those ever-present gales, seemed
to have lost their eeriness whenever I revisited our old beach to
contemplate our little white frame house, still standing but occupied by strangers. All that is left, in a material sense, are the sepia
photographs of our family in those happy days.

Thank God, however, not every treasure in life is a material
one. I still have my memories, an enduring trove, which I hope all
who read these remembrances will share.

Bernard Diederich
Pinecrest, Florida
March 2002

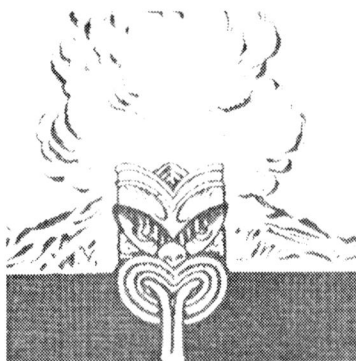

Be gone Sweet Ghost, O get you gone!
Or haunt me with your body one;
And in that lovely terror stay to haunt me happy night
and day.
For when you come I miss it most,
Be gone, Sweet Ghost!

Oliver St. John Gogarty.

CONTENTS

INTRODUCTION

They call it God's own country. But as a child, I often believed that God had failed to bless our small corner of New Zealand and that the Devil and all his malevolent allies had taken control of this disturbing end point of land. Today New Zealand is known as the place where the movie epic, *The Lord of The Rings*, was made. Remarkably, one of the locations in which it was filmed was Makara, our family's wind-whipped niche of New Zealand. Makara was truly J.R.R. Tolkien's Middle-Earth, and we children could easily have been mistaken for barefoot, red-cheeked, happy Hobbits. Makara though was full of both beguiling beauty and intimidating ugliness; it could be at once forbidding and friendly, insulating and liberating.

Notwithstanding its paradoxical setting, Makara Beach was our childhood sanctuary where my brothers, sisters and I shared in coping with the forces of nature, while escaping the worst of the economic maelstrom of the 1930s known as the Great Depression.

Summer in Makara could be heaven. Daisies, buttercups and red clover blanketed the paddocks. Foxgloves and honeysuckle grew by the roadside, and there were even clumps of yellow daffodils on the hills. Freshly mown hay was the most exquisite perfume. Our river's surface bustled with ducklings and goslings. The beach itself, giving way to the deep blue waters of Cook Strait, was warm and hospitable.

Gone during summertime was the iodine odor of seaweed dragged from the deep by the angry winter's sea. Skylarks and yellowhammers were everywhere. Sedately the kingfisher perched on a bough over the river before the Hawkins' swing bridge, contemplating its next meal near the water's surface. The big bumblebee arrived along with the flowers. Fly swatters were active and the sticky yellow bug catchers hung from kitchen ceilings were soon black with dead flies. There was no protection however against the ubiquitous, merciless, little sand flies.

For all the bedeviling insect life, we children roamed barefoot and free. Alas, nevertheless, a strong, bone-chilling southerly wind could quickly cloud those warm, glorious days of summer, sending us scampering home to seek shelter. We could experience all four seasons in a single day.

Winter, by contrast with Makara's summer, was raw, bleak and paralyzingly cold. The hills turned brown and then purple—the color of our lips—and took on the loneliness of a windswept English moor. The farmers, bundled up in gumboots and oilskins, were dark blobs on the horizon as they went about fencing their fields and cutting scrub. It was also when farmers shoed their horses. In sum, our rustic childhood romance with Makara had a touch of *Wuthering Heights*—enduring and tempered only by the wind.

A family, it is said, is a nation in microcosm. Our family nation was Makara.

When I began to paint this verbal remembrance of Makara I knew that my strokes and colors would evoke bittersweet memories of my parents, grandparents, of my two elder sisters, my three younger brothers and others from that long-ago family past. Like melded oils on an artist's palette, love and laughter are all mixed in with the melancholy that comes with reminiscence. During World War II, as a sailor in the middle of the Pacific Ocean, I had plenty of time to relive those early years at Makara. Since then, growing older if not wiser during a life that has taken me far from my homeland, I have had many an opportunity for further reflection. I have concluded that it is childhood and adolescence that defines us all, and I know how Makara defined—and helped make—me.

CHAPTER 1

From South to North Island

In the first days, in the forgotten calendars,
Came the seeds of the race, the forerunners:
Offshoots, outcasts, entrepreneurs,
Architects of Empire, romantic adventurers;
And the famished, the multitude of the poor;
Crossed parallels of boredom, tropics
Of hope and fear, losing the pole-star, suffering
World of water, chaos of wind and sunlight,
And the formless images in the mind;
Sailed under Capricorn to see for ever
The arc of the sun to northward.

A.R. D. Fairburn (1904-1957)

Our family had left Christchurch, the very English garden city in the South Island of New Zealand, for the capital city Wellington in the North Island in 1928. I was then two years old. It was the year that Charles Kingsford Smith, in an historic first, flew across the Tasman Sea—some 1,600 kilometers-between New Zealand and Australia—in his aircraft called the *Southern Cross*.

It is difficult for many if not most persons to recall the years before the age of four. So, much of what I know of the change of islands may have been told to me by my elders. And yet, I do recall the wonderful moment of departure on the inter-island ferry, when passengers threw seemingly thousands of colored streamers to friends and relatives on the dock bidding them farewell. The bond between ship and shore suddenly broke as the steamer pulled away from the dock.

Memories of the first houses we lived in after the move prob- ably come from being shown the dwellings later in my youth— very little changed in our homeland's original tableaux while we were growing up. (Many years afterward, however, most of the landmarks of my youth, which I sought to show my own children, had disappeared in the building boom of supposedly earthquake- proof edifices that occurred in Wellington after World War II.)

For a brief period we lived in Brooklyn (not to be confused with the New York City borough of the same name), a residential area perched on one of Wellington's hills with a spectacular view of the capital's deep-water harbour. Whether it was the terrain or the rent that was too steep for Dad—it was probably the combined burden of both—we moved down from the hills to the sea. So close were we to the sea at Breaker's Bay, around The Heads from Wellington, that we were almost awash in it. Facing the raw open sea Breaker's Bay lived up to its name, dashing up sheets of sea- spray that turned our more modest house into a dark and dreary place.

Brother Brian had been born 19 months after me (on April 26, 1928), bringing our parent's offspring to two boys and two girls. Two more brothers, Geoffrey and Patrick, eventually joined our little clan and Tony, a cousin, spent much of his boyhood with us. It was my sister Marquita (nicknamed Quita) a year older than me, who at Breaker's Bay gave me an early survival lesson. "Throw away those toys, Berber [the family sobriquet for Bernard]," she would command. I would obey. Then she would claim victory and sing: "Finders keepers, losers weepers!" As if on cue, the plump two-year-old I was at the time would burst into tearful wails. To keep me quiet she would be forced to return my toys. But her play taught me not to be so trustful.

To escape the unrelenting pounding sea, Dad decided to move from Breaker's Bay. A house was available at a place called Makara Beach, some fourteen miles from the city center. "Cities are dens of iniquity, no place to bring up a family," Dad never tired of extolling the virtues of the wide-open spaces at Makara. "All those bloody chimneys belching soot from the bloody coal," he would add, further defending his decision to move us to Makara. (Even though Wellington's status as New Zealand's "windy city" should theoretically have made its air quality among the healthiest in the world.)

Our father was an early nature-lover and he actually saw evil in human metropolises. He said they were centers of disease (specifically tuberculosis and diphtheria) and moral decay and warned us that perverts—whoever they were, he never elaborated—hung around public toilets in the city and preyed on children.

Working in New Zealand's capital city, managing a hotel, Dad indeed saw a lot of the underside of humanity. Although Wellington was not exactly the London of Charles Dickens, hard times had created pockets of poverty in all urban areas of New Zealand. Even in the countryside, because of low prices for their dairy products and wool, farmers were undergoing wrenching changes. Some, unable to keep up mortgage payments, had lost their farms. The good that came out of the 1920s and '30s was that New Zealanders were among the first to realize that, if they were to prosper, they needed the aid of science to improve the land and their farm herds.

Packed into Dad's fine, 4-cylinder, 2.7-liter engine automobile, a four-door Gray, piled high with baggage, we headed for this place called Makara. The trip took us through Wellington to Karori, a residential suburb where we bade goodbye to the city and motored over windy Makara Hill, the formidable boundary between town and country. It was still 1928, four months after Brian's birth, and in the years that followed, Dad was to make thousands of trips down that winding valley road to Makara Beach.

If Mum had had reservations over this latest move she never proclaimed it. But it was obvious that she found Makara less than idyllic and a terribly lonely place to be marooned. A young woman with a growing family, she was now effectively cut off from her own parents and friends in the South Island and its busy social life. Pictures in the family photo album testify that her former social life had been a very active one. However Mum's mother and father eventually followed us to Makara and others of Mum's relatives visited on the weekends and on holidays.

In the New Zealand of that day, whose one and a half million population was mostly rural, isolation was a way of life. Sheep farmers and their families lived on homesteads called stations, much more remote even than Makara. Our Makara house, for its part, was a modest four-room weekend bach as these small houses were called. It was around a corner from the beach and actually faced a river, not the sea.

The first known human settlers in the area, the indigenous Maoris, had long since quit the beach and adjacent valley, probably deciding, wisely, that Makara wasn't worth fighting over. The last Maori *"pah"*, or fortified settlement, was in South Makara. There had been another *pah* on the hill guarding the stream and flats beside Fisherman's Bay, and around the corner from our beach, where it was said the last of the gigantic wingless birds, the three meters tall Moa unique to New Zealand, roamed. Growing up we were always on the lookout for bones of the mighty Moa, and for greenstone axes and any other treasure the departed Maoris might have left behind.

To city folk back in Wellington, our moving to Makara made us country bumpkins, technically a rung lower on the New Zealand social ladder than even the urban middle class, and a reflection of the deep class-consciousness of the Motherland, England. Being from the countryside meant that you were less civilized, less articulate, self-conscious and classified as a "clumsy hoof." Yet, as transplants to the country we fell somewhere in between.

The "cowcockies," the small dairy farmers in the valley, at first didn't know what to think of us, as commuting to work in the city—which my father did—was unknown then. We were a race apart. But not for long. Dad and Mum soon befriended the cowcockies and their families and we became an integral part of the valley, which stretched from Makara Hill to the beach. They were mostly second-generation, hardy English farming stock whose parents had established agricultural homesteads in the valley only some seventy-five years before our arrival. There were also a couple of Irish families and one of Scandinavian descent. Our abode at

Makara, my father decided, had possibilities and it was not long before the banging of his hammer gained a regular rhythm and our house slowly, on weekends, began to expand. The smell of fresh paint soon mingled with that of frying sausages and fried bread. Dad's ceaseless domicile-enlarging process would continue for nearly 20 years.

Like his German-born father, he had a natural talent as a builder and could construct anything with his hands. He was not unlike the character, "Old Tarr," in an early Katherine Mansfield story set in Makara, not far from where the authoress once lived. "*Old Tarr*" was published in the *Westminster Gazette* of London in 1913 and the principal character, Jack Tarr, was a dairy farmer who, the story relates, had built one of the first European-style houses in Makara in 1870.

Like our father, Jack Tarr ("Old Tarr") spent an inordinate amount of his time erecting his house, obsessed all his life with its construction. But once he completed it—and here he differed from Dad—he felt he had intruded and despoiled the land. "His feet seemed to freeze into the cold grass of the hill, and dark thoughts flew across his mind, like clouds, never quiet, never breaking . . ." (A Tarr strangely enough lives today at Makara Beach.)

Authoress Mansfield's literary portrait of Makara was an accurate one, e.g.: "The great green shoulder of Makara Hill down to where the sea ran with a crashing laugh up Makara Beach and slipped back again, stealthy, quiet, and gathered together and came again, biting over the rocks and swallowing sand. They could snuff it in their nostrils and taste it on their lips."

Katherine Mansfield, who was to have such a powerful influence on the English short story, was, according to Dad, almost a neighbor. She had attended classes at the little red-roofed school at Karori Park at the bottom of Makara Hill. Her family had resided at nearby 372 Karori Road from 1893 to 1898, and we passed the lovely old wooden house where she once lived, called Chesney World, on our way to and from school. One day, while it was being renovated and turned into flats, my father told me that as he had passed the place, he noticed that the irreverent workers

had placed a toilet seat on the front of the building with a sign:
"K. M. sat here." The toilet seat and the sign were gone by the
time he returned in the evening.

Eventually Dad himself built three new rooms onto our house
and, too late for most of us children, added an indoor bathroom.
(Yes, we used an outhouse known as the long drop or dunny.) Dad
also constructed a game room over the detached garage, which he
reconfigured completely. Our tennis court—Dad decided we should
have a tennis court!—was a feat he accomplished by practically
scooping away the hill behind our house with the aid of an old
horse pulling the scoop. The Sunday Dad completed the work,
the poor horse lay down and died, the moment Dad unharnessed
it from the scoop.

Makara was truly "Down Under", near the bottom of the world,
on Cook's Strait, which Makara bordered. Some of the stormiest
waters on the planet separated Makara from South Island. On a
clear day the dark-bluish outline of South Island was visible on the
horizon. Nevertheless, the hardy Maoris were said to have used
Makara as a transit point to paddle by canoe between North and
South Island.

Topographically our Makara Beach barely resembled the rest
of the twin-island, Southern Hemisphere nation of New Zealand,
known for its verdant hills of extraordinary beauty and whose national emblem is the fern. At Makara hardly any of the lush native
bush had survived the local land-clearing process. Intentionally or
not Makara had come to look like the northern reaches of the
British Isles—we were a windswept, craggy outcrop of the "Old
Country." Though obviously misplaced, Makara's tough breed of
farmers had no qualms about reconfiguring their new surroundings to suit their needs. And so it was with some other parts of
New Zealand.

In fact Makara and the rest of New Zealand had once been
part of the southern continent of Gondwanaland adjacent to the
South Pole. Some two hundred million years ago, Gondwanaland
broke loose from its geological moorings and drifted away to its
own little corner of the South Pacific ocean, aloof and alone, some

1,600 kilometers (nearly 1,000 miles) from Australia, the nearest land mass.

On December 13, 1642 Abel Janszoon Tasman, the famous Dutch navigator, discovered what the Maoris called *Aotearoa*, "the land of the long white cloud" (or "land of the long daylight"), and christened it New Zealand. Mimicking Tasman's feat, we Diederich children imagined that we had discovered Makara in 1928, and we christened it "Land of the Wind."

CHAPTER 2

Those Makara Ghosts

While Makara represented a difficult transition for our parents—Dad was 29 years old and Mum was 28 when we moved there—it was a wonderland for us offspring, though a bit frightening at first.

My earliest recollection was the wind and the noises it produced. Our house was small but there was still plenty of room for ghosts, the bogeyman and Satan. Darkness fell early in winter and the light provided by the flickering fireplace in our front room, did not reach the bedroom which we children all shared. After a while, as the night took hold, the candles in the living room were lit. By now Dad had come home, and he would pump the gas lamp and carefully light the mantles. Although it still didn't reach our room, the gas light was a powerful ghost repellent.

"Cuddle up and go to sleep," Mum would say tucking us in after we had knelt and said our prayers. She then left with her candle for her and Dad's bedroom on the other side of the house, plunging us into darkness. Our guardian angel, she assured us, would provide all the light we needed.

Whether my guardian angel was a he or she I never learned, but whatever its gender that divine presence, as far as I was concerned, fell short of his or her assigned duty.

Fear permeated that inky blackness. With no reassuring nightlight we were at the mercy of wind borne, howling ghosts. They taunted us with their unearthly moaning and creaking. They alternatively whispered and screamed. The valley acted as a sound amplifier as these invisible phantoms would blow triumphantly out to sea. When they unleashed their full fury it would be a prize howler, a gale. Add thunder and lightning and your prayers were for an end to the pagan darkness!

The ghosts, for me, had all the attributes of spirits and beasts, and I was convinced they had their own language. I would try to reason with them, and when that failed and I prayed to God for help, the imagined wraiths turned crazy and joined a chorus of their evil-spirited friends to make life even more miserable as we huddled under the blankets.

At a very early age, during those winter nights in the darkness, as the phantoms raged out of control, I began to question my God's power as a protector of the small and weak.

The Maoris who had arrived in New Zealand some thousand years earlier had understood Makara's blend of beauty and hostility. That is why they had christened the place Makara, which in the language of the area's Ngati Toa and Ati Awa tribes literally meant: "Come; go; ahead. " Which could be interpreted as meaning, "Come to Makara, but go, head off somewhere else." The name ineffably reflected Makara's schizophrenic nature. The wind that we youngsters feared could not, we felt, be related to the Maori God of Wind, *Tawhiri-matea*; it was far too evil to be a god. It had to be the Devil. Had we broken a sacred *tapu* (taboo) by living at Makara Beach? Sadly in those days when we wanted to know more, we could learn so little of Maori mythology. It was much later that a Maori fellow student at Marist Brothers primary school told me about the mystical God *Mauri* and how he had caught the North Island with his grandmother's jawbone as a hook, fishing our land out of the sea. The South Island of New Zealand was his canoe. The "northerly" was the most ferocious wind at Makara. It could be unforgettably forbidding and frightening. My early environmentalist father was the only one I ever heard defend the "northerly." "The wind is good," he would say. "It keeps the air clean and we have the cleanest air in the world." Whatever its contribution, the wind to a major extent controlled our lives. Our home was protected to some degree by a small hill on which the spinster Cook sisters had built their house, which has managed to survive Makara's relentless weather until today. For a time their brother "Moldy" Cook and his wife Zelda lived there. They did not encourage visitors, as Mrs. Cook suffered painful piles and it was whispered that she had her own strange and alarming treatment. She was said to bath in kerosene or some fuel then available. The howling wind and driving rain often breached the hill. It was the northerly that made the sea progressively angry, snappy and rough. The sea would pound away at the beach with its big bluish-green fist which turned white with fury as it finally smashed into the sand. There was terror in the way each huge wave dragged away sand, rocks, and driftwood as it receded. The undertow was so powerful it could suck up a small human like a pebble and dump the body far out to sea.

Leaving bed and the hot-water bottle (central heating or an electric heater was unheard of, and we had no electricity anyway) for only a minute, to use the cold enamel potty under the bed or make the even more heroic five-yard dash in bare feet to the outside dunny, was asking too much of any child. Bedwetting, though unintended, lent a certain realism to that recurring nightmare in which I was engulfed by a giant green tidal wave. In the morning, faced with the soaking bed, my irate mother accorded me little sympathy. Even when I grew older, it was a true test of character to make the olympic dash out the side door through the wind, rain and dark to the chilly outdoor toilet.

In my recurring nightmare, a giant, apocalyptic wall of water would race across the Pacific (like the terrible tsunami that struck Japan in 1932), swallowing up all of us, towing us off to sea and dropping us off in freezing White Continent, the Antarctica. Childish nightmares aside, fear of the undertow off Makara Beach and a potential tidal wave was real, and from fear of such mighty forces came respect. My father recounted having had a close call with such a huge wave on the South Island coast.

As we youngsters grew older we would sometimes test the sea's strength by playing undertow roulette. We would walk into the water up to our knees and let a receding wave pull at our feet, but we would run away before it could suck us up altogether as in the nightmare.

At night when the beasts' howling diminished to a moan I knew they were getting tired. Yet long after the wind had died, the breakers would continue to crash onto the beach. Somehow in my young mind the wind and the sea harbored the same devils.

After the storm, seaweed torn from the bottom of the sea, and which for some mysterious reason smelled strongly like iodine, littered the beach. Smooth grayish stones covered the remaining sand. Odd pieces of flotsam and jetsam from the vast ocean were proof of the sea's power of destruction. A lifebuoy from an unknown ship that had met an unknown fate might take years bobbing its way to our shoreline. But the sea also brought little treasures. There was always an abundance of shells and stones polished smooth by the ocean's timeless hand.

The northerlies delivered our firewood in the form of driftwood. But once collected it had to be given weeks to dry out in order to burn properly in Mum's small wood—burning stove. On one beach-foraging expedition I found a coconut from some distant tropical island. (New Zealand is far too temperate for coconuts.) The "southerly" blew cold from Antarctica but it brought calmer seas. When the wind eased from either direction it was a heavenly relief. Yet heaven was always fleeting. For the Makaraites there was no east or west wind. Just the southerlies and notherlies that governed our lives.

Our view from the new front window Dad put in to give the living room more light was essentially a portrait of man's violation of nature—the destructive ecological footprint left by Makara's early English settlers. Their slash-and-burn techniques to clear the land for farming had left deep scars on the rust-colored, scrub-covered hills.

Still, nature had survived. Toitoi plumes and lupines waved beside the river. A solitary Norfolk pine which Dad had planted in the front lawn eventually flourished sufficiently to obstruct part of the dubious view. On December 25, just after the beginning of the Southern Hemisphere summer, that little pine tree became our living Christmas tree on which cheap Japanese toys were hung, as were my first boxing gloves and tennis racquet. The native pohutukawa tree, which Dad had also planted, provided masses of scarlet, powder-puff Christmas flowers. Yet the Yuletide scenes that we gazed at in our picture books were of snow and places and people so far removed from our own summertime celebration that Mum was forced to explain that the winterscapes were all created at "home" in England, where children like us had snow for Christmas.

A great emptiness would descend on Makara when, as sometimes occurred during our Yuletide season, the weather turned simply gray.

CHAPTER 3

Childhood Paradise

Our new home at Makara Beach proved to be a toddler's paradise. Later when I saw the drawings in one of author Beatrice Potter's children's books, the depictions gave a whole new meaning to the creatures under the waterfall a short distance from our house.

That cascading stream was a magical place where I recognized the frog sitting on the leaf of a water lily in the pond beneath the waterfall as Ms. Potter's endearing amphibian, Jeremy Fisher. Even tiny field mice became friends. Slimy Norwegian rats however sometimes startled us as they scampered along the river's bank. We hated them. Peter Rabbit kept a very low profile sensing perhaps that we often ate rabbits and hares for dinner.

The river was alive with Jemina Puddle Duck and her relatives. Sometimes an off-course wild black swan honked as it arrived on our river. Tall, dignified shags sat motionless by the side of our river, near clumps of flax. These sleek birds would suddenly dive under the water in search of a fishmeal and reappear somewhere else. The fables of La Fontaine, the French fabulist, such as that of the tortoise and the hare, seemed to come alive at Makara although we never did find a tortoise.

Stellamaris, three years older than I and the eldest of our brood, was in her childhood years the Devil's apprentice, despite her later closeness to God (as noted earlier, she became a nun). Whenever Mum went off to town to shop Stellamaris was left in charge. Her stewardship was especially scary during the dark days of winter. Outside, the scurrying clouds would allow the wintry sun to ap-

pear only in fleeting flashes. "Marla", as we called Stellamaris, would
begin the entertainment with "once upon a time" fairy stories and
update us on the adventures of elves and leprechauns. Then an old
Irish pagan ancestor would possess her and she would launch into
the most ghoulish and vivid ghost stories direct from the flickering
hearth of old Ireland. She would declare herself a witch and the
rest of us firmly believed her.

Huddled in a corner of the front room as Stellamaris hypno-
tized us with her eerie tales, we siblings would be too frightened
to move when darkness fell. All the while, smiling enigmatically,
our brass Buddha would gaze down on us from the mantle piece
over the fireplace. Stellamaris's imagination was matched only by
her acting ability. Yet, for all the goosebumps her ghost stories
raised, we preferred them to Peter Pan.

Our family boasted an RCA ("His Master's Voice") Gramophone
and we overworked, "San Francisco, open your golden gate . . ."
and other pop tunes of the era. (Eventually San Francisco did open
its Golden Gate bridge to me as my first landfall in 1943 after
sailing for 80 days across the Pacific on the four-masted barque
Pamir.) One autumn the Grammophone was broken; it was never
fixed. We youngsters were happy enough singing our own songs
and enjoying our own self-enacted plays and games. Stellamaris'
scary stories, which she made up herself, were always the main
feature. It seemed that her tales were forever heightened by the
accompaniment of a shrieking winter storm.

A cloud of dust on the unpaved Makara road—there was only
one road down the valley to the beach—would signal the arrival of
a very special visitor, the baker or the greengrocer or in summer
the soft-drink man. Unsurprisingly, the baker was our favorite caller.
We would quickly identify the baker's van and, rain or shine, rush
to greet Cooper's Bakery from town, at Karori. The baker would
open the back of his van and the smell of freshly risen bread and
buns was sheer ecstasy. The interior wooden shelves of the van
were lined with loaves, all kinds of buns and cupcakes, all fresh out
of the oven. We would look hungrily at the cream topped Boston
buns and cakes but the few pence Mum had given us for the baker

were for a big loaf of bread. "I want the bubble!" I would shout, and in accordance with a family rule the first to make a request won the right. (The "bubble" was the rich middle of the big loaf when it was divided.) We were always fighting over who had made the request first.

The greengrocer, a Hindu, drove an ancient Bedford truck laden with fruit and vegetables from throughout New Zealand. He always had some fruit the local farmers' orchards didn't supply. "Don't pinch the fruit," he would caution us in his wonderful inimitable Indian accent. The verb carried a subtle double entendre; "to pinch" also meant "to steal" in the language that both he and we had inherited from Mother England.

There was also another Hindu gentleman who came out in a vintage truck buying mostly old beer bottles. But as the farmers needed bottles for their own home brew, he soon stopped visiting Makara.

Collecting firewood was an early childhood chore. When we were not gathering it from the beach for our home we were helping the Hurlihy family chop, drag and roll manuka branches, too big and heavy to carry single handedly down the hills, to their home in the valley a mile from us. Often, while still very small, we tykes would lose our footing and tumble down a hill like Jack and Jill in the nursery rhyme. However, while roaming the network of hill paths created by the sheep and cattle we were assured of extraordinary adventures.

We refused to allow the wind to completely control our lives. In spite of that omnipresent beast, we began slowly to explore the wonders of Makara, venturing through its labyrinth of trails carved out by the foraging livestock. During such explorations, pluck and stamina were often needed to stand up to the wind when it blew sheets of salt spray in from the sea. One day, in midwinter, a lone penguin suddenly emerged from the river, believing perhaps it had returned to Antarctica as Makara's temperature was extremely low. The penguin paid us children no heed and waddled grandly up the pathway to the side of our house, where the flightless bird in its black-and-white tuxedo colors remained squawking until the next day when Dad carried it down to the sea. It swam away and never returned.

The incident was typical of Makara's Alice-in-Wonderland atmosphere. We literally jumped through the looking glass as squadrons of seagulls perennially wheeled and creaked overhead, riding the wind. When the gulls landed inland on old Hawkins' fields across the river, it was a sign that the beast would blow. We were warned never to throw stones at the seabirds, especially the big albatrosses which we recognized because of their giant, six-foot wingspan. They were *tapu* (Taboo) and Dad had told us about the Ancient Mariner. Like all good partly or wholly Irish Christians we were very superstitious.

On a winter night in June 1930, when Dad went to fetch Mum at the hospital and brought her home with the new baby, Geoffrey, I recall riding along and waiting in the car on a steep Wellington hill. Geoffrey was a big baby and he grew into an even bigger-than-usual young man, much taller than any of the rest of us, over six feet five.

Babies we were told were found in a "cabbage patch," so Dad had been to the cabbage patch at the hospital on the hill in Wellington. Someone else said babies were found under "gooseberry bushes."

The first sign of spring was the arrival of the lambing season. When we first saw those snowy-white newborn creatures, tails wagging and scampering over the hills, we wanted to play with them but they were difficult to catch. Though just arrived they could outrun us. Our first pet lamb, which we named Mary, we loved and showered with affection as one of the family. It got fat and playful and chased us. One day to our belated dismay, we ate Mary, learning of Mum's choice of main course only after the fact. Stellamaris pushed back her plate and we all followed, crying "how could you!" when we learned who our dinner had been. We cried. Mum assured us that there was no sin attached to killing animals for food—even sacrificing one's pet sheep. Abraham, whoever he was, had done it.

The lambs brought us our first instruction on the mammalian birthing process as did other farm animals that surrounded us.

Only once during my childhood at Makara did it ever snow on Makara Hill and even then the rare white stuff was quickly whisked away by the ever-present wind. In winter, however, frost turned the fields as white as snow. Rain knew no season, nor did the intermittent storms. At least once a year, and sometimes more, the river would flood and break its bank. It became a large, brown, swirling torrent causing great excitement and bringing bloated, drowned farm animals down to the sea like a grotesque carnival parade.

We had none of the "modern" conveniences that both of our parents' families had enjoyed. Wrestling with the small, ancient, wood-burning stove Mum somehow managed. A new stove was her greatest wish, but it was years before she received one. We children were given our baths in a galvanized iron tub set before the fire in the front room, a juxtaposition which was typical of rural New Zealand.

Both Mum and Dad were sticklers for cleanliness. In fact my father would rather find an excuse for not eating if we were invited to lunch or dinner by neighbors, particularly on a farm, and he decided that their kitchen was not up to his high sanitary standards. By the same token chickens running into Mary Jarvis's farmhouse during tea put me off her good food, especially when the chickens defecated on the kitchen's linoleum floor. It was not prudery. It was physical. I would become nauseated. (Mary was the kind-hearted wife of farmer Ted Jarvis who became one of Dad's hunting friends.)

Mum fought a daily war against dirt, and scrubbing the linoleum floor on her knees, she would command, "Don't bring the dirt in with you." We couldn't help bringing it in. We couldn't detach ourselves from it. We graduated from making mud pies in the back yard to becoming filthy running after that pot of gold which, we were assured, was at the end of the rainbow. We came close but never did find the end of those frequent rainbows that arched majestically over Hawkins' farm.

Mum really believed in preaching that old adage: "Cleanliness is next to godliness." (God had an honored place in our home and was cited often.) Civility also ranked high in our socialization process. "Manners maketh the man" was repeatedly emphasized. If one failed to add "please" to a request to pass the butter, there would be a severe reprimand and the butter would stay out of reach until an apology was given and the magic word uttered. Nevertheless Dad, who had been an altar boy in his youth, was I later concluded, a lapsed Catholic because he waited outside in the car while we went to monthly Mass at our church by the Crossroads. Mum did a lot of praying and had need of prayers in those early days coping with five small children (later to be six) and my father. She taught us to say the rosary. The earliest birthday present I remember receiving was a string of rosary beads and when I made my first Holy Communion I received another string. "Prayer is very important," Mum would remind us. And indeed I used prayer as my principal defense against my childhood enemies, mainly the wind and the many otherworldly forms it assumed. Making our first Holy Communion was the major event of our young lives. Fibbing was a terrible sin; even a little "white lie" was not acceptable. We belonged to the Irish Catholic church, the most conservative branch of the Roman church. James Joyce, himself a son of Dublin, had called the Irish "a priest-ridden, Godforsaken race." Our family believed in the Virgin Mary and penance but the fact that Dad didn't attend Mass engendered in me some early doubts about my faith. Dad never explained—nor did we ask—why he didn't attend Mass at Makara. In later years he did attend Mass regularly but that was after he had left Makara Beach to live in Martinborough where my brothers had their farms.

Our rustic playground expanded as our legs grew longer and stronger. There were miles of beaches, hills, gullies, paddocks, sheep sheds, shepherd sheds, milk sheds, orchards, the Makara River, and seemingly endless little creeks to explore, along with countless varieties of insect and other wildlife and sealife to study.

A small island directly in front of our house, in the middle of the river, was where ducks laid their eggs which, because of their strong taste, only Dad ate. We preferred to wait patiently for the ducklings to appear swimming behind their proud mother who glided along as queen of the river. On the island the eggs were safe from all the little imported egg-eating English predators, such as stouts, weasels and ferrets. The exception was the slippery rat.

The Baileys' home around the corner faced the full fury of the wind, but the family were closely tied to the sea. The Baileys—Phoebe, Dedee, Restin, and Nancy—were our childhood friends, but they seemed weighed down with all their fish chores.

There was a spooky cave on the climb around the rocks leading to Fisherman's Bay. It had become spooky after an important politician drove out from Wellington expressly to commit suicide in the cave. They said he had taken poison. Why this man had bothered to travel all the way out to Makara Beach to kill himself and haunt our cave was beyond our comprehension. We gave the cave a wide berth when we passed by, especially in the late afternoon or after dark. A clap of thunder would set us scrambling over the wet rocks at high speed. Quita was particularly frightened of thunder and flew over the rocks reaching home before all the rest of us.

The hills of Makara wore a bright and colorful coat in summer. The Scottish gorse and the New Zealand manuka flowered side by side, the unwelcome immigrant and the native competing with each other. While the lambing season was a sign of spring, haymaking was summer, the most glorious season of all. The wind carried the pleasant aroma of newly mown hay. The draught horses would be harnessed to the mower, and George Hawkins sometimes used an ancient hand scythe to cut the hay around the edges of his fields. The haymaking season sometimes fell during the Christmas and New Year holidays. My father would strip down to shorts and get a wonderful tan. My sisters and brothers also tanned. I stripped down and got terribly burnt, suffered blisters and became even more freckled.

Chimney smoke up the river announced the arrival of the Bach People. They were a race apart, but as "townies" and part-time Makara dwellers, they were very special and their love of Makara was genuine. The Bach People would suddenly appear in their little red bachs (houses) at the side of the river across from the

Hawkins' woolshed. The most dynamic of the Bach was Herb Hildreth who had discovered Makara as a youngster soon after the turn of the century. Even after he married Mollie they continued to Bach at Makara and came close to baptizing their two children Pam and Peter, in the river.

There were others such as Bill Spencer who took up residence next to the Bach People and became a fixture. His colorful language often made my mother wilt as she noted there were children present. He was a great builder and became my father's friend. His grandson Charles Graham at one time worked as a secretary at the U.S. Embassy in Wellington and later for the New Zealand Embassy in Washington D.C. and was a born entertainer.

A big tent would go up before the Monks' old red woolshed near our waterfall. One family of townies regularly spent their six-week Christmas holiday camped there. Camping was a way of life during the holiday season. Our natural playground would grow even larger. Now it could be measured in square miles.

New Zealanders tend to be outdoors people, and for us children the worst punishment possible was to be confined to quarters—"grounded" in today's parental parlance. Being forced by a family curfew to remain indoors, during a sylvan summer evening when daylight seemed to last forever, was true purgatory. It hurt more than all the ear-twisting, cuffs on the head, or spanking. (Corporal punishment was very much a part of our upbringing.)

How we fought against going to bed at the required hour in the summertime, when it was still light enough to play for so long and the Southern Cross (that unique celestial formation viewable from earth only in the Southern Hemisphere) was taking its time to emerge. Those were wonderful summer Makara nights. "Mum can we stay up, please, please, please?". "Can't we go to the beach? There is a haul tonight." How we hated any kind of curfew! A cardinal rule in any case was that we could never go out at night without first getting permission from Mum or Dad.

In the daytime it was different. The less our parents saw of us, as far as they were concerned, the better. Barefoot and free we ventured farther afield the older we got. There were no predators of humans in New Zealand, except the poisonous katapo spider which we rarely if ever sighted—and no human predators of the type that stalk modern communities.

In ancient times there were no mammals in the two island landmasses that became New Zealand. That explains why we ultimately had flightless birds such as the kiwi, kea and giant moa that were able to survive on the ground without taking wing. There was only one animal that we were warned about: the bull. Every farm had a bull and some were more dangerous than others. The Jersey bull in particular was untrustworthy. The stories of bulls' goring farmers, ripping open their gizzards, were only too real. We were extremely careful when we teased a bull. But tease the bulls (although we hadn't then heard of the Spanish sport of bullfighting) we did, and run we did.

Moreover the bulls, as did the rams, broadened our knowledge of sex.

CHAPTER 4

"French Louis"

Our beach was three minutes away by foot—if there was no wind to battle against. Backdropped by a high cliff, the beachfront began with a shoulder composed of smooth, gray stones uniformly round and no bigger than a man's hand which, in summer, retained the heat and burned our feet. After a storm the stones could be blanketed with driftwood and seaweed. Even the status of sand depended on the weather. A severe storm could suck the sand out to sea and replace it with stones. Then sometimes the sea would spew sand back onto the beach and then the stones would disappear.

It was safe swimming off the middle stretch of the beach. We steered clear however of the area where the Makara River poured into the sea. The joining of the two waters caused strange currents that carved holes in the sea bottom. Near the rippling river's mouth, and set back from the beach, were ancient sand dunes. The Makara Maoris reputedly used them in defending the area from an invading tribe. The dunes were our early sandpiles. They were also ideal for sunbathing and high enough to offer full protection from the wind.

Around a promontory from the beach was "Fisherman's Bay," a deep-water, protected cove where a colony of fishermen, most of them Italian, lived and kept their boats. You could smell Fisherman's Bay before you saw it because of its many fishing-related activities and installations, such as smokehouses. The bay was lovely and well insulated from the wind. So clear was the water that fish swimming thirty feet below the surface were visible. The fishermen's little homes, or tin whares, as they were called were one-room dwellings with a rustic stove and a chimney. They were built in a row against the cliff. A window was punched in the tin siding to provide a view of the boats at anchor and the maze of nets spread out to dry. All of the dwellings had small vegetable gardens in front of them growing mostly tomatoes. Detached were small tin structures, smokehouses in which the fishermen slowly smoked cod. Driftwood fires combined with the smell of olive oil, smoked cod and fishing nets gave the bay a highly pungent aroma.

The star personage of Fisherman's Bay was a non-Italian, known as "French Louis". He was a fixture with his long, flowing white beard seated before his whare with half a dozen of his fish-eating cats skulking around and fighting over a fish head. (The fishermen gave no thought to the "environment", nor did anyone else in the area except our father. Fish remains were strewn around everywhere.)

The old Frenchman's real name was Leopold Haupois, or at least that's what his neighbors said. His beard was quite remarkable—more impressive even than that of Santa Claus. It had turned yellow around his mouth where a pipe always sat. Despite his few possessions French Louis dressed with dignity and usually wore a dark suit coat. Word had it that he had arrived in Wellington in the French sailing barque *Beatrice* in 1878 along with a cargo of railway iron. Deciding to stay in New Zealand as a fisherman, he jumped ship to eventually become officially the first European settler at Makara Beach while it was still a Maori fishing village.

By the time we got to know him, French Louis was already an old man and had given up fishing. When he died in 1940, at a reported age 88, after the outbreak of war, Fisherman's Bay was dying too. French Louis used to swim across the bay and for us children that was a tremendous feat. Once he saved the life of an Italian fisherman who had fallen off his boat and was on the point of drowning. The picturesque character seldom ventured far from his whare. He would sit there gazing out to sea surrounded by his cats. He would however keep a critical eye on the manner in which the Italian fishermen repaired their fish nets and their crayfish pots. In his accented English he would talk of the times when crayfish were as plentiful as rabbits and six dozen crayfish would sell for less than a shilling.

There was something sad about this dignified man sitting there alone with his cats staring out to sea dreaming away his last days. The sea also played its symphony for him. It was my belief that French Louis had had an adventurous seagoing life and was now content to dream. We never knew for sure how old he was, but he was very old. He was a true Conradian character and I like to think he may have even sailed with the famous Polish-born sailor-writer.

French Louis took his dreams, figuratively cloaked in a strong northerly, to his grave. His choice of cemeteries shocked my mother, who knew he was a Catholic. The old sailor chose to be buried in the Anglican cemetery at the Makara crossroads. All we really knew about him, from his accent, was that his original nationality was undoubtedly French. He did tell us one time, however, that he was from Normandy, and as school children we knew all about the Norman invasion of England in 1066. He made no secret also of the contempt in which he placed his Italian fishermen neighbors.

It was paradoxical that in a valley populated principally by descendants of "pommies"—the pejorative New Zealand term for Englishmen—Fisherman's Bay was the domain of a dozen Italian fishermen and a lone Frenchman.

The Italian fishermen were all single men—at least they didn't have their wives with them— who had come out from Italy to make their fortunes, and who planned to return to Italy to marry or rejoin their wives, and live quietly ever after. The Depression years appeared to have interfered with their plans of making a fortune fishing in waters off Makara which were abundant with all kinds of maritime life. There was just no market for their catch. Alberti, a big Italian fisherman, became my friend. He played the guitar and sang in Italian and gave me my first taste of Italian food, fish fried in olive oil. One day pointing out to sea, he announced, "Over there is Italy . . . many miles. One day I return to Sorrento." Then he burst into a song about Sorrento.

Joe Volpicelli was also from Sorrento and had come to Makara in 1900 at age ten. He was the only Italian to break away from the ethnic isolation of Fisherman's Bay and move to our beach, to live with the Bailey family. The Baileys were fishermen and the only other permanent residents (besides us) of Makara Beach. When eventually the other Italian fishermen left Makara, Joe remained; he died at age 100.

He had liked to talk about the visits of the Governor-General, Lord Bledisloe, to Makara Beach and the time the high-ranking dignitary gave French Louis a bottle of whiskey. As soon as Lord Bledisloe left, French Louis shut the door of his little hut and downed the bottle, singing French, Italian and English songs to his cats.

We too met Lord and Lady Bledisloe, who evidently could not be kept away by Makara's intimidating wind. They were chauffeured out to the beach in a shiny black Daimler and exchanged pleasantries with us. There must have been something about the rugged coast that reminded his lordship of the British Isles because the old Representative of the King returned often before retiring to his home in England.

The grassy flatland in the little valley beyond Fisherman's Bay was cut by a stream, the fresh water source for the fishermen and campers. This valley had been one of the last refuges for the moa, a giant of a bird, standing as tall as a house with legs like lampposts and, like the kiwi, flightless. The valley was said to have been the Maoris' last hunting site for the moa. The great bird had disappeared seven centuries before Captain Cook discovered New Zealand in 1769. We liked to believe we had found a real bleached moa bone. It always proved to be an old piece of driftwood.

During those long, lingering summer days, "The Haul" was a main evening attraction. The Italian fishermen would come to our beach and row out with a huge net strung between two boats, mainly to catch fish for bait. They would drop it in the middle of the bay. Then they rowed to shore playing out the net on each side. Once ashore everyone would take their place on each side and haul the net in. We youngsters were allowed to help. It was slow work but fun. I was often given the job of coiling the rope.

We got wet but it didn't matter. Everyone sang the old sea shanties. The Italian fishermen had their own songs. But often as the line became taut and heavy, singing required too much energy and the rhythm was maintained with the shouted chant, "Heave ho, heave ho, heave."

When the net was finally dragged onto the beach, it was a magical mad mess of flipping, flopping and fighting fish of all types and descriptions. In their struggle to stay alive they kicked up a thick spray of sand and water. There would be a treasure trove of fish, exotic squid, sea horses, octopi and other creatures of the deep. We shrank away from the net when a messy blind eel was discovered.

The Haul was also the crowning social event of the Makara Beach summer, and under the influence of the moonlight, not all hands present on our beach were engaged in hauling in the net. Young lovers from the camping crowd were otherwise occupied.

When we were old enough to venture farther in exploring the coast, we found many a clue to unknown sea disasters, including pieces of ships. French Louis told us about ships that had gone down not far off our coast. He said, and we later confirmed, that the barque *Maria* had foundered near the beach in 1851 with 26 lives lost, and that the steamer *Penguin* had hit a rock off Terewhiti in 1904 with a loss of 75 lives. A lifeboat from the *Penguin* had washed up at Makara.

The Italian fishermen prayed for the southerlies, which would allow them to go out in their little launches and catch blue cod, snapper and grouper. The red cod often ended up as bait.

The Italians were also Catholic, but of a different stripe than the Irish. One of the fishermen openly supported Mussolini. When Mussolini, Italy's fascist dictator, invaded Abyssinia and the newsreels in the movie houses showed well armed Italian troops beating the brave primitively armed Abyssinians, Makara's Italian colony lost some local friends. The Italian fishermen were eventually moved during World War II to join anther colony of Italian fishermen closer to the city at Island Bay. There the authorities kept strict wartime control on their fishing. Overnight they had become the enemy. Italy had entered the war on the side of the German Nazis.

Several Italian fishermen known to be Fascist Black Shirts were interned on Sommes island for the duration of the war. It was a war that would change all of our lives.

The little bays and beaches along the coast were so completely deserted that Robinson Crusoe would have felt right at home. Stellamaris read Daniel Defoe and told us the story of the famous castaway, which we acted out. Given our childhood outdoor pursuits, only Stellamaris and Quita engrossed themselves in books, but I did discover *Treasure Island*, by Robert Louis Stevenson. (*Tusitala*, or the "Teller of Tales" they called him in Western Samoa, a group of islands north of us administered at the time by the New Zealand government. Years later I used *Tusitala* as a pen name and I was to become a friend of a relative of Stevenson, British author Graham Greene.)

One of the memorable events that occurred during our childhood was the arrival in Fisherman's Bay of a huge shark, close to where we sometimes swam. It had evidently been attracted by the abundance of castoff pieces of fish tossed into the bay after the fishermen cleaned their catch.

Uncle Brian liked to say that the water was as "clear as Bols gin," and indeed we could watch the shark swimming between the moored fishing boats in the bay. The shark was so big it snapped the biggest hook and line the fishermen could find.

Finally it was decided by general consensus that the shark had to be shot. My father volunteered to do the honors. Armed with a World War I vintage, Enfield rifle, standing aboard his launch in the bay, Dad waited. As the shark reappeared close to the surface, its fin just breaking the water, Dad took careful aim and with impressive accuracy blew the shark's brains out. A winch had to be used to haul the dead beast onto the beach. Its frightening jaw was propped open with a hefty length of driftwood and we all (including myself) posted for photos that were published in Wellington's *Evening Post*. When its belly was cut open it revealed several large fish that the shark had eaten whole. In the Depression-era economy in which little was wasted, the fish removed from the shark's stomach went off to market and were sold as "fresh fish."

Another day, while sitting on a rock with my legs dangling in the sea, I suddenly realized that a large object was headed for my feet. As I yanked my legs out of the water the mysterious interloper spread open tentacles like a fan, obviously searching for my extremities. It was a huge octopus not one of the notorious giant squid that was reputed to live at a great depth in the deep channel that passed through the Cook's Strait.

Farther along the coast, on the other side of the Makara River and opposite Fisherman's Bay, lived another Makara character. Tom Long was a true hermit. He lived alone and kept to himself in a house that resembled the skeleton of a prehistoric monster, because of all the sun-bleached driftwood piled onto it. Tom was obsessed with collecting firewood and he had enough, my father said, for a dozen lifetimes. He had already lived several lives, it was said, and in one he had reputedly been a swagman. Dad said, "Poor Tom, he's a little queer," meaning he did not enjoy all of his mental faculties. His being a little strange was the result of internment in a German prisoner-of-war camp. In his early life he had been a sailor and his ship had been one of the first captured at the beginning of the 1914-18 Great War by a German Raider.

Once we Diederich boys spied on Tom from the cliff above his strange, small home. We watched him gathering drift—wood, got tired and left. Only later did our father tell us that we had run a great risk as Tom believed the Germans were spying on him, and waiting their opportunity to take him prisoner again, and thus he had a gun to defend himself. One night he fired his shotgun at his clock, believing he was fighting off the Germans.

As we grew up we heard stories of the last Maori massacre (among themselves) which had taken place near the river's mouth and among our sand dunes. Legend had it that the survivors had hidden their greenstone battle axes and other weapons in a cave. We searched all the caves we could find but uncovered no such treasure. The Maoris were said to have placed a strong *tapu* on the artifacts, so when we didn't find them we were relieved. We didn't know how to handle a *tapu*.

The noted, the campers from the city were our regular sum-

mer visitors. They pitched their tents in the valley, or near the
sand dunes at the mouth of the river. We were very possessive of
our sand dunes and the tussocks! We didn't like the idea of strangers baking their bodies on our sand. It was our important annual
rite. We never wore shoes at Makara even in the coldest days of
winter. Like the Maoris before us we lived off the sea and the land.

The ocean continually replenished the miniature aquariums
in the huge rocks in the bays and inlets along the coast with water
and little fish. We thus had scores of natural fish ponds.

Shellfish were plentiful. Mussels, pipies, paus and tuatua could
be dislodged from the rocks at low tide. We could eat them raw
(there was no fear of pollution in those pristine days) or boiled in
the billy on the beach, or take them home for dinner. We never
tired of examining the vast variety of colorful seashells. Some we
could put to our ears to hear the secret moaning of the spirits. It
was a world filled with endless surprises. So fascinating were the
beaches that it was impossible to remain indoors with so much
adventure waiting outside.

In sum, our childhood universe was a world apart, set in deep
isolation, but with the distant world washing up on our shores.
We even found seashells in the hills which proved they had once
been under the sea. In vain we searched the seashore for ambergris,
which we were told was priceless. When we were told we were
searching for whale vomit used in the making of exquisite perfume
we called off the hunt.

CHAPTER 5

Of Waltzes & Weddings

Looking down from the top of Makara Hill to the dividing line between the city of Wellington and the countryside on a summer's day, one found the contrasting views startling. On one side the scene was of neat, multi-colored suburban homes and the rich green park peopled with little white-clad figures playing cricket, croquet or bowls. The park at Karori, a suburb of Wellington, had been created in 1911, after the big totara-tree forest, which previously occupied the expanse, had been felled. When the Wellington tram lines were later inaugurated, the park became a terminus. The city stopped at Karori. Coming home from visits to Wellington, we reminded ourselves that the Karori general store at the bottom of the hill was our last chance to shop; there were no shops at that time on the Makara side of the hill.

On the other side of the landscape, the view from Makara Hill was one of wild and haunting beauty. Spectacular. Rugged, lonely, windswept hills rolled down to the sea. Even sheep, a permanent fixture on the typical New Zealand landscape, were not plentiful. Poly Angus and Hereford cattle searched for patches of grass among the Scottish gorse that was in the process of swallowing up the pasture land.

Shortly after our move to Makara, the Wellington city council had a ten-feet-high concrete wall built on top of Makara Hill to serve as a windbreaker and to keep cars and bikers from literally being blown off the road. Before the wall was constructed some cars had been tossed like a summer salad into Makara's deep gullies below.

With axes in hand, the early British settlers had chopped, slashed and burnt the native face off Makara. They labored hard to clear the land of native forests and huge trees to make way for pasture land on which to graze their dairy herds. What little of the beautiful native bush that remained had been overlooked in the deep crevasses between the hills.

Scottish and English immigrants, seeking to remake the New Zealand countryside into an image of the "old country," introduced into the new colony the prickly, thorny bush known as "gorse" that was utilized as natural fences in Scotland and even used there and in Ireland as fodder for horses. While it was easily trimmed and controlled in Scotland, in New Zealand the gorse literally ran wild, gobbling up the land wherever the import was planted. There were also local *manuka* and *tarwini* to compete with the gorse and the English broom plant. The gorse's only saving grace was its pleasant scent when in bloom.

It was still hungrily running riot in Makara when we moved there and the sons of the early immigrants were hard at work again clearing the land, this time of a menace introduced by their forefathers.

Those descendants of the original immigrants became our neighbors and friends. Our closest neighbor, a mile up the road, was George Hawkins. His father had come from England via Nova Scotia in the family's own ship. George was a gruff, elderly cowcocky—i.e. dairy farmer—who was severe with his only full-time farmhand, his son Jack. Jack in turn was a rough-tongued sourpuss.

Old George doted on his pretty daughter Iris. His wife Nellie was warm and friendly and in her later years increased her nip of gin a little too much. Life in the Hawkins house revolved around their kitchen. Their front room, as in most farmhouse parlors, was filled with their best furniture, which was also very old; they even had a piano, which was seldom played anymore. The parlor exuded a museum-like quality. There was a little porch at the back of the house where the rubber gum boots and oilskins (raincoats) were left. In rainy or sunny weather entry into the kitchen was in stocking feet. My father still wouldn't eat in their house, especially with his sensitive nose couldn't stand the odor of old socks. He always proffered polite excuses. The kitchen was also, for him, too close to the cows.

Others in the valley included the Monk, Cook, Jarvis, Robinson, Duffy, Trotter, Gaskins and Bowen families. Their forebears had come to Makara as early as the 1850s when land was cheap. Once they cleared the native bush they established dairy farms and hauled their milk and butter to town by bullock teams and later with draft horses. (The Cook family owned the land on which our house stood and ran sheep on the hills behind our house. The red wool shed along the road past the waterfall belonged to them.)

By the time we arrived in Makara milk was being transported to the pasteurizing plant by truck. But also by then Makara's farms were on the decline. Scrub-cutting had become an expense that many local farmers could ill afford, and in the years that followed they slowly lost the battle against their own "old country" weeds, conspicuously the gorse. Many farms were literally shrinking. It was also more costly to compete, since the farmers had to adopt new scientific methods of top-dressing the land with the right kind of fertilizers. Makara's proximity to Wellington had in itself once allowed these farms to prosper. But the days of the oxen cart were over and the Makara's dairy farmers could no longer compete against modern transportation and the big corporate dairy farms.

Not far from the bottom of Makara Hill, at "The Crossroads," where the road to Makara Beach branched off to South Makara, was the war memorial. The Crossroads was the spiritual heart of the valley: St. Mathias Anglican Church sat on a rise overlooking the cemetery and, dominating the scene, gave The Crossroads the appearance of an English village. The church had been built in 1921. The war memorial listing those from Makara who had died for King and Empire in World War I was surprisingly long for such a small community.

Our Roman Catholic church, Mum was proud to say, was there first. Set in an open field some 300 yards up the valley from The Crossroads, the simple wooden structure had been inaugurated on Sunday, September 7, 1873, and dedicated to St. Patrick. Its stained-glass windows depicted the saints, whom I got to know intimately during those long, once-a-month Sunday Masses.

A short distance up South Makara Road from The Crossroads was The Hall, a wooden community building. The Hall was Makara's social center where romance blossomed during dance nights that often led to a wedding in one of the nearby churches, and a reception, which was naturally held in The Hall. Besides being the local terpsichorean center The Hall served as the school hall and church hall, hosting social activities of both institutions. Accompanied by an accordion, we youngsters all learned to dance the fox-trot and waltz on The Hall's highly polished wooden floor. On a stage at the far end of The Hall, my acting career began at age six and ended almost simultaneously when I suffered an attack of stage fright during a school play.

On a hill behind The Hall sat the Makara public school. It was a high-ceilinged, three-room, wooden building surrounded by trees that made it an oasis from the wind. It had been built in 1874 and was destined to become our little red schoolhouse. The structure was actually only partly red—the rest was painted in cream and chocolate colors. It was surrounded by beds of marigolds and geraniums.

A wooden gate at one side of The Crossroads led to the Hislops' house. Covered with vines, the cottage was dark and creepy. It served as the local post office when we took up residence in Makara, and old Mrs. Hislop would hand out the Royal Mail on her doorstep.

She may have been a nice lady, but I never waited long enough to find out. Her surroundings convinced us children that she was indeed a witch. But in those days the mail was scant—letters, directed to Makara were few and far between. Those that did arrive were addressed to the recipients simply in care of "Makara Beach." There were no street names or house numbers in Makara, much less zip codes.

As a youngster, I was curious to see the inside of the Anglican church, but our family's strict Catholicism made it a sin to enter any house of worship other than a Catholic church. The list of sins in the family's Roman faith was a long one. It was even a sin to question the validity of a sin, or to question our faith or any of the church's teachings. Fear of committing a mortal sin was a terrifying thing that made one feel the heat of Hell's fire. Even at Makara, God was Irish and Hell was real.

In an Irish Catholic family, religion was then by inoculation at birth. No member of such a family would foolishly question their faith or the existence of God. We weren't silly. Of course there was a God. We all believed in God. I wouldn't think of not going to church. The consequences were too dire to contemplate. The Devil already had a foothold at Makara Beach, just as I believed he was in league with the ghosts in our house.

Father Herlihy, who later served as a chaplain in World War II in the New Zealand forces, in North Africa and Italy, along with our Uncle Roy would come out from Karori to say Mass once a month at our Makara church. He became a family friend. (However I found that going to confession before Mass at Makara was more difficult than in a big church in the city where you were anonymous. Father Herlihy knew all the voices of his little congregation whom he was confessing at Makara. It could be embarrassing even to confess to little fibs.)

There were only a few Irish families in Makara, but they were prolific enough to fill half the pews in the little Catholic church. Captain Monaghan for instance was an early settler in South Makara with a large family whom we met in our small church.

Mass was once a month and enjoyable only in the dead of winter when it was too cold to be outdoors. As I grew older I began to fret at the length of the Mass and I wasn't the only one who agonized over the priest's long and often boring sermons. He was not reaching me. He was monotonous. I had difficulty concentrating. If it was summer I left my mind at the beach. But while very young I needed prayer, especially to fight the demons that came with the wind on dark and stormy nights.

Each time Dad didn't attend Mass I feared he was risking being struck down by lightning. One mortal sin and you had lost your admission to Heaven for eternity. *"Hors de l'Eglise, point de salut,"* was a saying in French—"Out of church there is no salvation." Yet the beauty of our religion was that if you sinned you could go to confession and have it wiped off your moral balance sheet.

A friend contended to me much later in life that Protestantism made you into a hypocrite because, according to his interpretation, Protestants claimed both the "right to the pursuit of happiness" and the right to sin. Non-Catholics don't have the privilege of the Catholic to sin and later be washed clean by confession or by special indulgences after attending many Masses. As a consequence, my friend's theory went, Protestants sin (in the pursuit of happiness) and then dissimulate their sinning which is hypocrisy. During the Victorian age, secret sinning was a vogue.

The Hurlihy family, despite the fact that they came from Ireland, didn't go to church. Maybe they had no way of getting there since it was a good eight miles away from their household. They had no farm and rented an old house about two miles from us with a Model-A Ford tin-lizzy rotting in the garage. Tim Hurlihy spoke with a heavy Irish brogue and he was the Makara roadman. He worked usually with Art Hawkins who did a spot of shearing also during the wooling season, but couldn't find other work. Together they would clear any minor earth slides or shovel the gravel back and forth across the road. It certainly was not backbreaking labor, although Tim would always be on the road in even the worst weather. "Ganger," Mr. Tim once told me, was the name of his kind of workman in Ireland.

Tim and his wife may not have been Catholics, at least they were not practicing Catholics. Mum, therefore, was a little skeptical of them. Nonetheless Tim was a good if quiet man. When we were attending school, we would meet him every day on the road as he was bicycling to work or smoothing out the gravel with his shovel. He would always greet us leaning on his shovel. The deep gravel he and Art Hawkins piled up was a hazard to our bikes.

The Hurlihys' house was surrounded by scraggly microcapa trees. The place also had a little bamboo forest at the river's edge.

We children would help the Hurlihy boys gather firewood which was, for every Makara family, a never-ending task. In the clumps of trees bordering the road we went bird-nesting—searching for birds' eggs—which we collected until we had an extensive variety.

When I grew older Tim's son Desmond Hurlihy introduced me to an even more adventurous pastime, tickling trout. Years earlier someone had placed some brown trout (as so much of New Zealand's flora and fauna, the species had been imported from England) in a little stream up the hill on the Giddings sheep station (farm). It was a sport that I found difficult to master. Brown trout sometimes rested during the day in the shadow of the bank that overhung the stream. Desmond would work his way along the bank on his knees with one hand in the water. Suddenly his eyes would begin to roll signaling contact. He would lie on the grassy riverbank with one hand submerged in the clear water and slowly and softly stroke the stomach of the fish. Soon after making contact and with the trout evidently enjoying the tickling, he would close his hand on the unsuspecting fish and swiftly flip it out of the water to land a good distance from the stream. I never did master the sport and pretty young Daphne Hurlihy, Tim's youngest daughter and one of my earliest crushes, objected to my carrying tickling into our childhood relationship.

Nor did we like all the customs of the English. On one of our early Guy Fawkes Day celebrations at Makara, we made our Guy out of hay, and pushed him around in a pram singing, as they did in the city, "Penny for the Guy, hang him up high, hang him on a lamp post and let him die." But there was no one to give us any pennies at Makara. Nonetheless we had the biggest bonfire of the year on that November night. Poor Guy. Mostly hay and dressed in our castoff clothes he was placed on top of the huge stack of firewood on a little bluff at the river's edge. Once lit the bonfire turned into a raging outdoor furnace fanned by the wind. Some of us children, while still too small to appreciate the concept of adult revenge, became attached to our Guy Fawkes dummy and were upset by the burning of our newfound friend to the crackling of firecrackers. (Observed annually in England and by expatriate

Englishmen on November 5, Guy Fawkes Day is a macabre festival that is celebrated by the burning in effigy of the man who tried to blow up the British parliament in 1605.)

CHAPTER 6

Rugby Played Cupid

It wasn't long after we had settled in Makara that Mum's father, mother, and brother joined us there. They ensconced themselves in a house they constructed next door to us. I often wondered whether Mum had sent an SOS to Grandpa Jim McCleary, and Nana, *nee* Margaret McCarthy, to help in coping with our growing family.

They arrived, along with Uncle Brian—a nationally and even world-famous boxer and rugby player, who was to become our resident coach—in a big Nash roadster. It was a fabulous automobile with room for eight. It had two dicky seats that could be pulled down. It had a canvas top and a big wooden steering wheel. They said it had been custom-made for someone, who couldn't take delivery, so Uncle Brian had bought it new. Only in winter was riding in it shock treatment. It was like a flying ice box as wind penetrated its canvas hood and window flaps.

Grandpa McCleary had himself been one of New Zealand's early champion rugby players, and he had also been a major influence on the form of rugby played in New Zealand. He was born in Auckland on July 19, 1863, becoming the first native-born New Zealander in our family.

It was also rugby that had led to romance between my maternal grandparents. Margaret McCarthy, our grandmother who was to become Makara's matriarch, was 22 and already a superb seamstress, when she met the dashing rugby footballer, Jim McCleary. Unlike Grandpa, Nana was not born in New Zealand, having come out from her home in County Cork, Ireland, with her family as a young girl on a sailing ship in the 1870s.

Precisely how Jim McCleary met Margaret McCarthy in Wellington—it was a small town then—whether at a rugby match or social event after a game, or in some other circumstances, they never said. They met, fell in love, and were married in Wellington's St. Mary's of the Angles Catholic Cathedral on July 23, 1888.

The McClearys were Northern Irish Protestants and, given Nana's strong Catholicism, she made Jim convert to her religion to marry her. The matter was never discussed among us and Grandpa was not at all formally religious.

Their honeymoon was at that time a novel one: they spent it in Australia on an historic rugby tour. As captain of the Alhambra Rugby Club, Jim McCleary led the first New Zealand team to play overseas, and the setting was Australia. They remained in Australia long enough for Grandfather to be invited to play for the Victoria team.

(When after seventeen years in Makara they celebrated their (diamond) wedding anniversary at the Karori Parish Hall, the messages of congratulations they received included greetings from the King and Queen of England; Sir Bernard Freyberg, the Governor-General of New Zealand; and Mr. Peter Fraser, the New Zealand Prime Minister.)

Even in his sixties Grandpa was a fine figure of a man who, in his earlier years, had developed what became known as "the New Zealand style" of rugby football. We liked to think of Grandpa as one of the undisputed fathers of New Zealand rugby, which indeed he was. Two of his sons likewise excelled at our national sport. Son Brian was not only a member of the All Blacks, our famous national team, but had played with the celebrated 1924 All Blacks, known as "The Invincibles" because they had won every game in their tour of the British Isles, Europe and North America. Uncle Brian had also been Australasian heavyweight boxing champ.

The new house that Grandpa, Nana and Brian settled into had a washing shed at the back with a bathtub and large copper boiler. This meant that Mum could now boil our clothes in the

big copper boiler and scrub them in the sink and bathe us in style.
We graduated from the small tin bath to the full-size bathtub next
door. It was our job to find kindling wood and start the fire; in
that drafty washing shed coaxing the wood to burn was no small
feat. Then we would ladle the steaming hot water from the copper
boiler into the bathtub. In wintertime, however the water was
soon only lukewarm. I shared my bath water with my brothers.
How we dreaded bath night next door in the dead of winter! Hopping over the wood fence was fine, but dashing home to bed after
the warm water bath was a traumatic shock to the nervous system.

I can still see my Grandpa McCleary sitting there in the wall-
papered kitchen next to the stove under a thick halo of smoke from
his big, curved Peterson pipe which rested on his chin. I was seven
years old and we loved Grandpa. He was kind and often gave us
some of Nana's sweets—blackballs they called the sugary candy—
and that's often why I was there in the kitchen.

A huge man, with a Norse nose and the large craggy head of a
Viking, Grandpa also enjoyed Scotch whiskey and cigars even in
the darkest days of the Depression. His chair, specially built, was
slightly elevated, like a throne. It had been custom-made to fit his
large frame with plenty of room for his old rugby legs. Above the
stove was a framed photograph of the American boxer Jack Johnson,
in a pose with his two fists raised. But Grandpa's great love was
rugby.

My younger brother Brian, whom we called Baby Brian (to
distinguish him from Uncle Brian), spent a lot of time listening to
Grandpa, who was a good storyteller as well as a *bon vivant*. Grandpa
could talk about every important rugby match during his adult
lifetime and about playing the game in Otago in the South Island.

I didn't have my brother Brian's patience. I got bored with all
the talk of rugby, people, towns and places I didn't know, mostly
in the South Island. Grandpa's jokes were worth listening to once,
but he often repeated them. Like Jack London, whose stories I had
the opportunity to read, I preferred the call of the wild. The outdoors were more appealing to me than the indoors, and Grandpa
spent a lot of time indoors in his declining years.

Outside, in winter, even if the sun was shining it was cold. Nevertheless I would go tramping over by the river at the Hawkins' place behind the woolshed. A slight stinging sensation remained in my mouth after munching too much watercress. I would eat it fresh, first dipping it into the crystal-clear cool water. Watercress grew in abundance there.

When provoked Nana could get her Irish up and if she had been faster on her feet we would have gotten a lot more walloping. When we broke one of her house rules she would chase us with Grandpa's leather belt intent on giving us a thrashing. A domineering Hibernian matriarch, she had beautiful, snowy white hair, which was almost the color of her fair Irish skin that couldn't take the sun. I had no doubt that she was really Bridgit, the Druid goddess who had managed to make the transition to a Catholic saint. Nana told us about an ancient Danish earthwork fort adjacent to her family home in a rural part of County Cork. Indeed her eldest son was christened Brian in honor of Brian Boru, the man who had defeated the Danish invaders of Ireland in 1014.

Blessed with a fabulous memory, Nana described in great detail the location of her childhood home. When, years later, in 1954, my mother and I visited Ireland, we found Nana's family farm and its big house, with a long, thatched roof, in a place called Ballein Gany, near the towns of Newtown and Charlville in County Cork. Sure enough the remains of the Danish fort she had described so well were exactly where she had placed them on her map. Our immediate McCarthy relatives no longer lived there. The only kin in the area, who resided not far away, were Katie and Nan Maher, sisters who were distantly related to Nana.

Nana's family had survived Ireland's Great Famine of 1845-50 caused by the potato blight, during which more than a million and a half of the Irish perished from starvation, cholera and typhus. Another two million were forced to emigrate, principally to America and Australia. (New Zealand at the time was still very new and only a few emigrated there. Nor were they welcome as immigrants for a time by the authorities in New Zealand.) However, by the time my mother and I visited, Nana's ancestral farm, her branch of the family had almost disappeared because so many of the sons and daughters had become priests or nuns. Mum filled a vial of earth with sod from Ballein Gany to take back to Nana in Makara.

I can still remember the nostalgic childhood scene at Makara: Nana McCleary would come in and bend over the stove. The scones needed another few minutes. She would close the iron door and the sweet smell of baking would fill the kitchen. Nana was preparing Grandpa's afternoon tea. The redness of his big nose was a sign that he had already had a nip or two of Scotch whiskey upon his return from his daily walk to the beach. It was there that he would spend long periods leaning against the big white rock that distinguished our section of the beach, and observing the sea. The white rock stood apart on our beach, like a veritable geological albino in the sand, and was set near a jagged outcropping of black rocks that separated the beach from Fisherman's Bay.

Grandpa, like French Louis, could gaze at the sea for hours as the waves caressingly accompanied his dreams of those vanished days of glory on the rugby field. It was after his walk that he had need of a stiff whiskey.

Both Grandpa and Nana had been accustomed to the social and sporting life of Dunedin and Christchurch. If there was a party or dance in Makara, Nana would attend and not leave until the Maori farewell song ("Now Is The Hour) was sung and officially ended the evening's entertainment. Grandpa didn't attend such functions, however, in Makara at least, and while Nana after going with us wouldn't dance, she never tired of watching others enjoy themselves.

Nana doted on Grandpa as well as on her eldest son Uncle Brian, who had fallen in love with a German girl in occupied Germany at the end of World War I, but after he left her behind, had never married. Brian talked little of the terrible trench warfare in France but he recalled when his troops entered the city of Cologne at the end of the War and captured a German General in a smart gold braided uniform only to learn that their captive was a postman.

Occasionally Grandpa would go to Wellington and no matter what pub he entered he was always recognized and someone was always shouting him a whiskey. His humor was vintage New Zealand, and dry Irish. His philosophy personified unflappable dignity. He would tell us, "Don't take off your coat to work or to fight." Grandpa also had his idiosyncrasies. If, as our neighbor, he needed salt or sugar, he would toss a stone onto our roof to attract attention. If you didn't have what he wanted he would turn in disgust and mutter, "They never have anything in that house."

Upon his death in 1949 a newspaper noted, "Jim McCleary's old club is generally regarded as having developed a rugby organization the like of which has never been seen in the history of this country."

The rugby football pioneer was also seemingly a pacifist; he would not permit Uncle Brian to go off to World War I as a combatant. So, reminiscent of Ernest Hemingway, Brian participated in the Great War as a soldier by driving an Army ambulance in France and later in Germany. Grandpa never mentioned, nor did we ask him, what his aversion to military life stemmed from. We believed it was rooted in his father's years of soldiering in the Imperial British Army. However Grandpa would seldom talk of or glorify his father's military career, and didn't want any of his sons continuing the military tradition.

Living in a land of the present, not the past, we children were more preoccupied with growing new roots. Nevertheless we were to learn years later, thanks to Stellamaris's research, that the legendary stories about our maternal great-grandfather, who had been the first of the family to arrive in New Zealand, were more myth than reality.

There was no dispute about the fact that shortly after Queen Victoria declared New Zealand a Crown Colony and thus a member of her vast Empire in 1840, John McCleary, our maternal great-grandfather, arrived in the new colony as a member of the British Imperial Army. He was a big Irishman over six feet tall, with an enormous bushy beard, and family lore had it that because of his height he had become a member of the Queen's Own Regiment, or as his papers state —Royal Artillery.

According to one family version, John McCleary, a member of the Imperial Army, had arrived in Auckland in 1842 having been sent out by Queen Victoria. He was one of twelve six-footers (or "fencibles"—whatever that meant) to take up land in Wellington, but had preferred to stay in Auckland where soldiering opportunities were better as well as the money. This version further alleged that our maternal great-grandfather had died for Queen and Empire in an accidental munitions explosion in Auckland in 1876. As it turned out, however, such was hardly the heroic case.

Ironically, the year of John McCleary's death was the year our German paternal great-grandfather, Casper Diederich arrived in Wellington with his family from the port of Hamburg.

Our military ancestor John McCleary had a two-story house built at 23 Alten Road in Auckland in the 1850s, where Grandpa McCleary and his six brothers and one sister grew up. Grandpa recalled that, as children, he and his brothers used to slide down the hillside behind Alten Road on cabbage tree heads, to be scolded by their mother who had to wash their clothes. There was no running water in Auckland then, and the boys had to fetch water daily in tins that they balanced at the ends of poles. The city's Scottish church, St. Andrews, was built nearby in 1848-1850.

John McCleary's four other sons, our maternal great-uncles John, Edward (Ned),Thomas, George and Richard,were known in Auckland, along with their lone sister Annie, as gifted amateur performing artists. Edward (Ned) was a tightrope walker, Thomas was a ventriloquist, and Richard a tap dancer. Ned and George would string a rope across East Street between lamp posts and all the neighbors would gather to watch the free show. The talented McCleary boys put on a lot of free performances and became involved with the early theatre in Auckland. Jim, our grandfather was more interested in sports.

It was an effort in 1970 to save John McCleary's old house (which was to be destroyed to make way for yet another motorway) that led Stellamaris to uncover the real story of our maternal great-grandfather's demise.

Stellamaris had become a nun in 1946, and eventually returned to her old school, St. Mary's Convent in Wellington, as art director. She had become involved in trying to save old houses and other historical buildings. During her research she did an etching of a little two-story colonial house next to the Auckland University campus that was doomed by a planned motorway. Her sketch turned out to be a rare coincidence. She discovered that the house had belonged to none other than our great-grandfather John McCleary. She went on to help in the fight to preserve it as an example of early Auckland architecture. (Its place in history had indeed been recorded, albeit not in a manner consistent with heroic idealism.)

With her etching completed, Stellamaris wrote to the National Archives Department of New Zealand's Internal Affairs Ministry asking for all the details on file concerning John McCleary. Their reply to her inquiry in 1970 can be summarized as follows: "

Born in Lurgan, County Down, Ireland, John McCleary was the son of Thomas McCleary, farmer, and Margaret McCleary *nee* Johns; he was married, aged 25, at Lurgan, to Elizabeth Smyth; he had lived in New Zealand sixteen years at the time of his death— which suggests an arrival date of 1859 or 1860." Yet his wife Elizabeth's death certificate gives her arrival date as 1852. She died at age 65 years. At the time of her death she had sons aged 45, 43, 42, 40 and a daughter aged 38. The fifth son, Richard, was born on May 17, 1860, and James, our grandfather, on July 19, 1863.

As for his military career John McCleary had indeed come from Northern Ireland to New Zealand in the Imperial British Army during the Maori wars. He had however arrived with the 18th Foot, a line Regiment, and was later transferred to the Royal Artillery.

Nor had John McCleary died in a munitions explosion or at the front of his troops fighting Hone Heke or Te Rauparaha's forces during the Maori wars.

The official document which Stellamaris obtained, and which was entitled "An inquisition indented, taken for our Sovereign Lady the Queen," turned up that Great-Grandfather McCleary, who had left the Army in 1870 and was receiving eight pence a day as a pension for "third degree" wounds, died on the 26th of January 1876 from accidental self-poisoning by carbolic acid!

The testimony of Thomas Johnson (publican), of the Windsor Castle Inn (a pub), states that Great-Grandfather, "being in a state of mental obfuscation from the effects of alcoholic liqucor [sic] on the 26 day of January in the year 1876, at his own house at Parnell by mistake did drink and swallow down, a certain quantity, to wit, about two drachues [sic] of carbolic acid, being a deadly poison; and immediately after became sick and distempered in his body and of the said poison taken as aforesaid, and . . . within a space of fifteen minutes after swallowing said poison, did die . . . the jurors aforesaid, upon their oath aforesaid, do say; that the said John McCleary in manner and by means aforesaid by mistake and misfortune did kill himself. . . ."

An addendum attached to the findings of the investigation stated: "The jury desire to express their opinion that the drug known as carbolic acid being a deadly poison, should be inserted in the schedule of the 'Poisons Act of 1871.'

Great-Grandpa McCleary had at least made one known contribution to a young New Zealand. By tragic accident, he had forced the government to place carbolic acid on the nation's list of deadly poisons!

Stellamaris had written that he was buried in Symonds Street Cemetery behind the Jewish Cemetery in a grave under a big tree, without a headstone and with only a wooden paling which rotted away with time. His wife, our maternal Great-Grandmother Elizabeth Smyth McCleary, had remained in Auckland for only a short time after his death. As most of the children had married and moved to other parts of New Zealand, she decided to join son John in Wellington, where she died to be buried in the Karori cemetery.

During a visit to New Zealand in 1998, and while staying at the Sheraton Hotel in Auckland, I discovered an old cemetery in a gully across the busy thoroughfare from the hotel. It had long since been closed for burials and many of the names on the headstones of the pioneers and early settlers had been erased by time.

Those names that remained were difficult to decipher. Capt. William Hobson, R.N., New Zealand's first governor from 1840-1842, had a simple slab of white marble. As for Great-Grandfather McCleary an Auckland librarian explained that I had been searching in the wrong cemetery. In those days, even in death, there was separation by religion. Our great-grandfather, hailing from Northern Ireland, was an Anglican, and his resting place was on the other side of the Sheraton Hotel and over grown with lilies and native bush. It was directly behind the Jewish Cemetery. The tombstones of those early Jewish settlers were in much better repair than the headstones of other religious groups.

Curiously, a week later while I was on a visit to Wellington, the Karori Cemetery sexton directed me to Great-grandmother McCleary's grave. In place of her tombstone there was an impressive tombstone in remembrance to her husband with the emblem of the Royal Artillery. So great-grandfather John had gotten his head stone after all.

CHAPTER 7

A Cowcockie's Life

Despite my running nose, bleeding knees, and torn pants, as a tyke I wanted to be a "cowcockie". Each of the Hawkins' cows had been given a name by old George and I soon knew them all and they knew me. At age six I had summoned enough courage to ask Mr. Hawkins' permission to help at the cowshed.

My life as an apprentice cowhand began one winter by sweeping the cow manure out onto the dung heap next to the road, where it frosted over and stood as still as the big rock candy mountain. Preparing the cows for milking was the next step up from manure sweeping, although on a dairy farm it's impossible to escape the manure.

There were all kinds of old wives' tales that adults expounded on to children. Pinching each other for example was bad because it caused cancer. If we ate the healthful crust of the bread our hair would curl and we all wanted curly hair. To grow tall all that was necessary was to stand in cow or horse manure.

As I was then up to the top of my gumboots in cow manure I was bound to be taller than my father who was over six feet. I ultimately reached six feet two inches.

Standing tall in the manure I next graduated to rounding up the cows and driving—more like escorting—them from the pasture to the cowshed yard. Before dawn I would run up to the Hawkins farm and fetch the cows from the paddocks. The cows knew the routine and plodded obediently along to the cowshed from the hill or from across the river. The dogs were always there to help in the roundup.

Not all the cows responded to their names. Some had to be pushed or otherwise persuaded to enter the bails in the milkshed. Hay awaited them at the head of the bails and once they poked their head in they were locked in by closing the bail on their neck. One hind leg was stretched back and tied with a rope as was the cow's tail. Washing the udder and tits came next.

Eventually I graduated still further to a small stool from which I could also milk the cows. It was a great privilege and I enjoyed the work. The milk was poured into an old-fashioned separating system and then into ten-gallon cans which the milk truck carted off to town.

Like everything in farming there was an age-old method to the art of milking. Sitting on a little stool, head pressed against the side of the cow, you either pulled or squeezed two of her tits in quick succession to produce a steady stream of milk into the bucket held at an angle between your legs. It took coordination and some practice. The animal, depending on its character, would either continue munching hay or kick. Several tested me by kicking the bucket of their milk out from between my knees; one particularly shifty cow put its dirty hoof into the bucket of milk. "What's the bloody hell wrong with you turnip-head," old George admonished me in his colorful argot. Adding, "you silly bugger."

Another danger was that cows are not toilet-trained and they considered the milk shed as good a place as any to do their business. Some defecated without warning; it sometimes plopped into the milk. Needless to say hygienic conditions in that cowshed were not the best. But in those days no one thought to question the quality or biological value of Hawkins' milk. Milk was good for you and I got to drink a lot of it.

Gruff old George suffered a bad liver and devoted his whole life to farming, working seven days a week the entire year and never taking a vacation. And I wanted to be a dairy farmer like him! Because of his rough-hewn manner I often wondered later whether old George had been any relation to the famous John Hawkins, the British seafarer contemporary of Sir Francis Drake.

George's son Jack was unpleasant enough to have been the son of a bad-tempered pirate. Jack was cruel to animals, especially the dogs and the cows. He could milk cows faster than a machine could today but I hated his treatment of the cows. When a cow was uncooperative he would grab its tail and, with a quick movement, snap it like a stick. All of Hawkins' cows eventually had crooked tails, Jack's trademark. Other farmers often cut their tails off. He would also kick the cow, and any of the sheep dogs that were expert in bringing the cows in and out of the yard, if the dogs did not obey his whistle.

In addition to its name, each cow I found had its own personality which I associated with people I knew. I took care not to divulge such bovine associations to the human individuals involved. Nor did I care about being paid; indeed I was not paid. The privilege of working on the dairy farm was recompense enough. When hay-making time arrived I might be rewarded with a few shillings but I was quite content to work for free. It was enough to be accepted as having the makings of a future farmer. Work was a great pleasure. We youngsters didn't think in terms of money; it didn't have that much importance, as our lives had many other compensations.

Sometimes I would be invited to breakfast, a robust affair, cooked by George's devoted wife Nellie, a good-hearted woman. Jack, I believed, hated farming and was often annoyed by the pleasure I took in my work. When he returned from World War II and service with the New Zealand army in North Africa fighting General Rommel, Jack became a barber. I often wondered how he treated his customers.

Years later I visited a monument in the little town of Brightwater, near Nelson that was dedicated to Lord Ernst Rudoford, the first New Zealander to win the Nobel prize for science. Recognized as the man who split the atom, I discovered had he like me had begun life milking cows.

There was no ritual as rich or exhilarating as hay-making. With a pitchfork it was possible to sculpt a haystack. It was a bit like constructing a house and when the haystack was completed it was as big as a house. Hay was pitched up from the back of a horse-drawn wagon to top off the haystack.

Eventually I rose in rank even higher to the horse-and-rake which was a little like driving a trotter at the races. The hay was scooped up from the field and then you had to pull a lever and pile the raked hay in a near perfect row. Raking took coordination and speed. Overconfident at the end of the day I chose to enter a field gate far too small to accommodate the big farmer implement. An iron wheel of the rake hooked onto the gatepost, the horse panicked and galloped off across the field with me bumping along on what was left of the handsome hayrake to the general amusement of the holiday crowd and anger of farmer Hawkins.

Old Tim Hurlihy, when helping with hay-making at the Hawkins', used the ancient scythe. But most farmers in the valley by that time were utilizing the horse-drawn hay mower, a mean-looking machine with sharp steel teeth.

Hay-making began after milking in the morning. We stopped for "smoko" (which was not only the time to roll a cigarette and smoke it but more importantly it was a break for biscuits and tea); later came a picnic lunch; then afternoon smoko and finally late-afternoon tea, which was actually dinner. All four were splendid meals spread out on the field by Nellie, her pretty daughter Iris, and other female relatives. It was strenuous work and the piles of sandwiches, slices of mutton, buns and cakes were considerable.

The horses were majestic animals. I would ride the old farm draft horses bareback and long for the day when I could ride a "real" saddle horse, not just a farm animal. But the farm animals were our real toys. Just as well.

Money was in short supply during those Depression years. There was no such thing as an allowance then or later. If you wanted money you had to work for it. Dad kept his job as unemployment in the country rose to a disastrous level and, like our little river, the Depression figuratively swept many souls away to sea.

In fact as we grew we spent more time on the river and even ventured out to sea. We had a small dinghy called the Corker, and quickly learned to manage the oars and row. Later Uncle Brian acquired a larger open boat with an outboard motor in which we used to go fishing at sea. I would get terribly seasick. Coming back from fishing, we tied the boat up in front of the house.

I preferred the river to the sea, farming to fishing. The river bank belonged to us. It was an extension of our front garden. The river water was then quite clean. When the tide was in we could row up the river past the Hawkins farm and as far as the Neilsons, where the water narrowed into a stream. When there was no wind we would row out the river's mouth into the sea. It was tricky and thrilling maneuvering into the sea at the river's mouth. It entailed pulling hard on the oars in order to avoid being swept back onto the beach on one side, or the rocks on the other.

CHAPTER 8

Mutton, Mutton, Please Pass the Mutton

At Hawkins Creek the area's best watercress grew. Wisely we examined the creek to make sure no sheep had died near where we picked the watercress and drank the cool, crystal-clear water which we considered almost as tasty as the water from our well at the foot of the hill behind our house.

We hadn't heard of a refrigerator and meat and butter were kept in a "safe," a little wooden box hanging outside the house so the wind could keep the contents at least cool. The only ice we knew of was that which covered the fields and puddles during a freezing winter's night and we made no effort to utilize it. Dad and his mates drank their beer warm.

Becoming really famished while exploring the Hawkins hills, we would be chased by the cows whenever we tried to share their field of turnips. We even learned to eat the heart of the wild thistle, another prickly weed imported from Scotland. The Irish hadn't brought with them the various species of "green bread," plants they had subsisted on during the famine years, so our choice of field salads was limited.

In the early evening it often fell to me, the apprentice farmer in the family, to fetch the milk. Three pennies' worth filled the billy at the Hawkins' and I would walk the mile home swinging the pail, which had no lid, over my head without spilling a drop. It was my early education in centrifugal force. The milk-fetching chore later fell to younger brothers Brian and Geoffrey.

During the shearing season the countryside suddenly came alive. Long white ribbons crisscrossed the hills as hundreds of wool-laden sheep were mustered. On the Hawkins' farm the sheep were driven by the dogs to a drafty old red woolshed. Mustering sheep was another farming skill and teaching the dogs to obey was rough on the vocal cords. "Come in behind," was an order to the dog to retreat and crouch behind the shepard.

Shearing was one of the hardest tasks. Each sheep was forced into a sitting position while Jack Hawkins and his father clipped off the wool with hand shears. Again Jack had little concern for the welfare of the animal. If he sliced a piece of flesh off with the fleece, too bad. The poor ewes, naked and bleeding, fled the young butcher.

My job was to clean and superficially grade the wool—if it looked good, it was good—and pile it in the wool press where it would be cranked down into a hefty bale. Each bale was branded with the farm's name and numbered and eventually hauled across the river by horse and cart.

The docking and dagging season was hardly appetizing. Dagging entailed clipping clean the dags—shreds of matted or manure-coated wool hanging on the sheep's behind. Docking was something else. Young Jack Hawkins and his father used the most primitive method of removing the male lamb's testicles which Jack called "denakerizing." Expertly they sliced the lamb's pouch open, then in a split second removed the testicles with a quick bite of their teeth and spat them out. The remnants of the little lambs' masculinity were piled high near the railing against which the Hawkins performed their surgery in the wool pens. It was quick, bloody and disgusting and one farming job which I declined.

Each week the Hawkinses slaughtered a sheep under the trees by the wool shed. Again it was primitive butchery. They would slit the sheep's throat, let it bleed, and then skin the animal and hang the carcass from a branch of a tree. The routine varied in the summertime when blow flies would attack the meat. It was then wrapped in a fine white material called mutton clothes. Male calves suffered an especially brutal end. Old George or Jack would use the blunt side of an axe to stun the frisky calf and then slit its throat. The calves (veal) went to the dogs. There was no room for veal on our preferred menu featuring mutton, meat from mature sheep.) Both the skin of the calves and sheep was kept and sold to tanneries to be made into leather goods.

In spite of the "Great Depression," there was no shortage of mutton on our dinner table, except on Friday. As the "Prods" (Protestants) used to sing, "Catholic dogs stink like frogs and never eat meat on Friday." On holidays Mum cooked spring lamb and spring potatoes served with fresh mint sauce. (Treasonably my Haitian-born wife suggested years later that New Zealanders didn't know how to season lamb and used mint sauce to hide the strong taste!)

At Makara we never tired of eating lamb hot or cold and in many forms. The meat grinder was an essential part of the kitchen. Ground mutton produced a species of hamburger although we had never heard of the traditional American version. Saveloys—a sausage with red skin—were a treat but I was never endeared to black pudding as blood sausage was called. Rhubarb and prunes were an important part of our diet and I was forced to eat parsnips, which I hated in every form.

(During World War II in the Pacific, while serving with the U.S. Merchant Marine on an oil tanker, I caused a minor mutiny by almost ordering a diet of prize New Zealand lamb for the crew. The detail I had led ashore for supplies at the U.S. base in Milne Bay, New Guinea, realizing that I was in awe of a warehouse stacked to the roof with tons of the best Mount Egmont prize lamb, and about to fill our order, shouted in chorus, "No way, no way!" The Americans aboard ship hated lamb. I complained to the chief cook. He shrugged. Then I took the matter up with the captain. "No cook in this war, at least on our side, knows how to cook lamb or mutton except perhaps a limey and we don't have any aboard," the captain said laughing at my disappointment. He suggested I wait until the war was over to satisfy my appetite for lamb.)

Growing up in Makara, we children received no sex education from either of our parents. Nature was at work all around us. One of our lambing seasons taught me about childbirth and also put me off meat temporarily. We had found a dead ewe lying prostrate on a narrow hill path with a dead lamb halfway out of her womb. George Hawkins explained that the ewe had rolled onto her back and it couldn't right itself because of its heavy coat of wool. Blow-flies were already collecting on the dead ewe and its stillborn lamb. It was a tragic sight that has remained with me ever since. And even with my enormous appetite I couldn't face eating mutton for weeks.

Opossum hunting was another sickening business. An ugly creature under the best of circumstances, when skinned, this marsupial was even more dreadful. The Australian brush-tailed variety—introduced into New Zealand during the last century—from Australia loved its new habitat, and our country's opossum population exploded. Opossums had even colonized Makara. Some farmers made an extra bob or two by selling the animals' furry skin that were used in the manufacture of fur coats. Even today this unwanted immigrant remains a threat to the native bush. Blessed by its isolation New Zealand had, apart from a couple of bats, no mammals. It was a land of flightless birds and rare plant life. The gigantic Kauri trees in the North island were said to be two thousand years old. But many of them fell to the axe for use as ship's masts and spars. The British Navy had a special interest in the timber and native flax, used for making rope. It was often said the main reason Queen Victoria decided to make New Zealand her colony was her Navy's need for a new source of rope—flax!

CHAPTER 9

Makara School

Protesting all the way, at age five I was taken away from my more serious pursuits at the beach and enrolled in Makara School at the crossroads, which was indeed a long way in those days.

On my very first day, I whistled in class and was sent home with instructions to return the following year, which was fine by me but not with my parents or my pro-education sisters who were in part responsible for my conduct. The whistling was to cover my nervousness. My sisters had inadvertently helped build up my anxiety with their concern for my education. They would often warn me after I had committed some stupidity, "Wait until you go to school!" I soon equated the restrictive nature of school with Hell. Stellamaris and Quita were both doing well at school and were to excel throughout their academic years.

In New Zealand's culture of that day, put-downs of others were almost a national trait. Life was tough and people vented their feelings of frustration or inferiority by putting others down, including the young, just to feel better, which is of course one root cause of prejudice. Thus our whole growing up process seemed only to reinforce an inferiority complex. It was a rough-hewn rural New Zealand society where compliments were rare and rancor seemed more commonplace than happiness. Farmers would taunt youngsters with nicknames drawn from the child's failings or physical appearance. If the head was large, he would be "Big Head;" if the feet were too big, "Big Feet." Seldom did his correct name echo over the fields.

After a while I answered to all kinds of names: Blockhead, Big

Feet, Big Head, etc. My being big for my age gave farmer George Hawkins a whole repertoire of appellations (in addition to "Turnip-Head"). When I complained to Dad, he said, "Better big feet than small ones and anyway you have a bigger grip on New Zealand with those big feet of yours than they have."

Holding my breath and keeping my lips firmly closed, I went back to Makara School at age six in 1932. Unbeknown to me at that tender age, it was the worst year of the Great Depression in New Zealand, a year that produced food riots in Dunedin, Auckland and Wellington. I promptly fell in love with the teacher, pert Miss Sherm. If I had whistled then it would have been in appreciation of Miss Sherm.

Primer 1 was not Hell although I still faced class with a considerable trepidation. However, an early extracurricular activity eased the tension. Miss Sherm needed free laborers and sent a couple of other farm boys with me to dig soil and plant marigolds around the fringes of the lovely old high-ceilinged school.

Each morning we were dropped off at the bottom of the hill by Aunty Madge who drove us in the Nash. We hopped over a turnstile and ran up the hill to the well-lighted classroom filled with tantalizing books and charts. Aunty Madge, one of Mum's sisters who was living at the time with Nana and Grandpa next door, along with her son Tony, was to learn, while driving us to school one day in Grandpa's Nash, that she could not smoke and drive at the same time. The lesson came when we sailed off the bridge at Gaskins, the huge car landing on its side in the Makara stream. It was the event of our young lives. We had been in an automobile accident, rare in those days, and survived without injury! Also there was remarkably little damage to the sturdily built Nash. (Two of Mum's other sisters, Hilda and Doris, were living in Wellington. Both had married men who returned from the Great War [1914-18] with physical wounds and psychological scars too deep to allow married life to work. All three sisters, including Madge, my "favorite aunt," had separated from their husbands by the time we arrived in Makara.)

Madge spent a great deal of time with our grandparents and

ultimately permitted her son Tony to remain with them in Makara. She later lived at 62 Pirie Street, in Wellington, with Uncle Frank, Dad's brother. The relationship was never discussed. Hilda lived at 22 Bolton Street, also in Wellington, and at various times we children stayed at both addresses when we were involved in college exams or playing football or cricket.

School notwithstanding, my preference was still the outdoors, not the classroom. There was an exquisite strip of native bush near the school and our Miss Sherm took us there on nature study trips. It was one of the last sizable stands of native bush at Makara and it attracted the remaining native bird species such as the tuis and pigeons that fed on the wild berries.

Following Miss Sherm, as we entered the coolness of the canopy of ancient native tree ferns, we would hear the distinctive but rare call of the bell bird, a native tui. This oasis of ancient evergreen shrubs and trees was once, we were told, the home of the kiwi and other rare birds who fell prey to the predators brought to our country by the immigrants. That was a school class that I loved! Miss Sherm was obviously an early naturalist and I decided that I wanted, besides being a cowcockie, to be a naturalist.

It was thrilling to listen to my pretty teacher describe our country's bountiful natural setting, but there was never a word against the settlers who had destroyed most of it especially in the Makara region.

I would later read accounts at the old Turnbull Library across from Parliament describing ships with manifests listing birds from the British Isles. I never really forgave those early colonizers who, for reasons I still can't understand, brought out to New Zealand shiploads of their partridges, pigeons and troublesome blackbirds, starlings, thrushes, redpolls, and linnets as well as goldfinches and yellowhammers. A whole avian menagerie was sent out in the mid-1800s. New Zealand had plenty of its own beautiful native birds, but the London-based "Acclimatisation Society," which sponsored the shipment of birds, obviously wanted to remake New Zealand into a South Pacific England.

And I had been a victim of one of those immigrant birds while "bird nesting", which was one of our earliest sports as children. High up on a micracapa tree one day, I was reaching into a nest full of eggs, when a magpie came screeching out of the heavens and pecked me on top of the head causing pain and blood to flow. This magpie, of British or Australian descent, made me lose my footing and I bounced down to be caught on lower branch. The incident hardly endeared me further to the winged colonial imports.

With Miss Sherm—whom I remember as trim and petite with lovely black hair and blue eyes—I learned reading, writing and arithmetic after a fashion and passed my exams. But my deeper learning experiences remained outside school. An example was the abundant cache of sea shells which my siblings and I discovered one day high on the cliffs, hundreds of feet above the sea, that told us that the hills were once under the sea. Clearly we were born geologists!

However my lovely teacher didn't see me as a budding scientist when I was caught dissecting a beetle. Deeming the post-mortem a disgusting act, she sentenced me to having my mouth washed out with soap and water, a punishment usually reserved for children who uttered swear words in the classroom or school yard. The fact that she herself administered the punishment was the greatest humiliation.

While classes at Makara School have mostly faded from memory, the annual school picnic I recall with clarity. It was a wonderful country fair and a remarkably happy and well-organized event, the highlight of the academic year. There were pony races, egg-and-spoon and sack races, plenty to eat including a cornucopia of toffee apples and other sweets. There was also no end to the soft drinks.

Nonetheless I still fault Makara School for ending my acting career. (I had the starring role in Chicken Little.) The school play opened at Makara Hall, the plain little building that had managed to keep the community spirit alive through peace and wars, and had also been the site of so much budding romance. But there was no romance in Makara Hall for a big-for-his-age six-year-old that day. Covered with yellow feathers I had been stricken with stage fright the moment Aunty Madge put on my first feather.

After all these years I can still see the expectant faces of proud parents and relatives—except my Dad who, mercifully, was at work. As they pushed me onto the stage The Hall appeared huge, the audience enormous. I had memorized my lines, or at least five words. The great moment had arrived. The words didn't. They were on everyone's tongue but mine. My tongue was frozen. The whole audience began prompting, repeating out loud my lines. When I finally stammered, " Run, run. The sky . . . "The Hall exploded into laughter and I ran offstage in a burst of quivering feathers.

Aunty Madge said I brought down the house with applause and laughter, but I saw nothing funny about my performance and in fact died a thousand deaths of embarrassment afterwards whenever I remembered my debut.

Swimming and kindred childhood sports came more naturally than acting. We began dog-paddling in the river during our fourth summer at Makara. As we got bigger we moved to the sea and first Dad, and then Uncle Brian, taught us in the ocean how to do the Australian crawl. In chest-deep water Dad had a way of swinging us onto his shoulders, where we would stand and then dive into the surf. It was great sport. He and Uncle Brian were both strong swimmers. The New Zealand Amateur Swimming Association was extremely active in turning schoolchildren into proficient swimmers.

I recall receiving my first proficiency certificate from the association in 1938 as a student at the Marist Brothers school and another later at St. Patrick's College. With our 3,200 kilometers (nearly 2,000 miles) of coastline and many rivers, it was essential that all New Zealanders learn to swim.

Only rarely did Dad join us for rugby, and the one time he did, it was disastrous as he put his foot through our ball during a kick. And whenever my brothers Brian and Geoffrey and I decided on a wrestling match it would soon turn from laughter to tears, from fooling to fighting. Geoff was usually the first to lose his temper, screaming, "You stupid cow," or "Silly cow!" (It was customary to refer to each other pejoratively as "cows" in rural New Zealand at the time.)

Once I shot Geoffrey in the behind with a little air rifle while playing on the bank of the river. The projectile was a little lead pellet and it left only a red mark. He retaliated by throwing a penknife at me. Amazingly it was on target and pierced the back of my leg. Fortunately neither of our wounds required cleaning or even the usual iodine cure-all.

At night Geoff would eat apples in bed, something I couldn't stand. His teeth biting into those apples grated on my nerves much like scratching on a blackboard. Then he would sing hymns. Brian, for his part, had a sardonic sense of humor and was more of a philosopher and loner and very good at math.

A memorable experience in tramping over the many hills that surrounded us came when I was eight and Brian seven. We went on a camping trip by ourselves that turned out to be more of a survival course. The trip was supposed to have lasted a week or so. It lasted half of that as two hungry boys came home.

Dad had let us off in the hills at the Giddings' sheep station. We walked off into the sunset and Brian suddenly disappeared. Made top-heavy by the backpack that towered over him, he went tumbling down the first steep hill. His fall turned our supply of breads to crumbs.

We nevertheless explored down to the coast toward Te Kamara Bay and then along the coast to Terawhiti, the largest sheep station in the region. When we reached the sea the only sustenance we could catch were spiny sea urchins. They were not exactly a delicacy. Still concerned (from my nightmares) about a monster tidal wave I suggested to Brian that we sleep at a comfortable distance from the pounding sea.

Still, exploring new beaches and hills during our camping adventure was exciting, and we eventually came upon a stretch of land scarred by a phony gold rush in 1870. There was still rusting, abandoned machinery standing which had been used in the search for the precious metal. Makara farmers later told us that a callous early day con man had literally triggered the gold rush by "seeding," which was done by firing a shotgun loaded with gold into the side of a hill. He then sold his "claim" at a handsome profit and disappeared. The area, they said, had indeed yielded 273 ounces of gold, but it was hardly enough to sustain a "gold rush." However, the incident had brought life to South Makara. There had even been a hotel that was called the Miner's Arms. It had offered meals, entertainment and facilities to wash clothes. We climbed over the rusting old mining machinery that remained as testimony of the country's love affair with gold.

Given our hunger when Brian and I arrived at the old mining site, we wished the hotel hadn't closed in 1894, two years after the "gold rush" ended. Finally returning homeward from our long march famished, we found a paddock of turnips and munched on them along with the grazing cows.

CHAPTER 10

Rescuing the Kia Ora

It was about this time that our family acquired "a real boat," a "real beaut," we called it. The nifty 30-foot fishing launch was named *Kia Ora*, Maori for "Hello."

The launch had been wrecked on the rocks off Te-ika-a-maru which had been Anglosized to Te Kamera. The owners had abandoned it. Pat Smith, manager of the huge Terawhiti sheep station on whose rocks the craft had foundered, told Dad, "You can have it, if you can get it off those rocks." Mr. Smith was a well-educated Englishman, the offspring of an old well established family back in Britain who had been shipped off to the colonies. He was a good friend during our years at Makara and gave me my first horse, Ginger, which Geoffrey later claimed as his.

Dad had no trouble talking his hunting mates into helping salvage the Kia Ora. Pat Carmody, an Irish-born jeweler in Wellington, and farmers Les Monk and Ted Jarvis joined in the memorable project, which quickly became the talk of Makara.

They managed to get the boat off the rocks and beach and remove the engine at Te Kamara. Then, with the canvas from an old tent that a group of Salvation Army hikers had abandoned on the shores of Te Kamara Bay, Dad patched the great hole in the boat's kauri-wood hull. They strapped four big empty, but airtight, oil drums to the craft's hull, and then, with our fourteen-foot, outboard-motor-powered dinghy, they towed the *Kia Ora* along the coast from Te Kamara during a southerly.

Keeping as far out to sea as possible to avoid the rocks, they pumped and bailed water out continuously and—the worst tribulation of all—they had time for only a couple of beers. It was, Dad recounted, a race against the sea and the wind, all the way. "If the wind had changed we would have been sunk," Dad used to say in recalling the famous voyage.

After the craft was pulled ashore at Fisherman's Bay, Dad went to work with his carpentry tools and the rescued derelict was seaworthy in no time.

Regularly Dad, Uncle Brian and their friends would spend Sundays aboard the vessel, deep-sea fishing. The rehabilitated *Kia Ora*'s inboard engine produced fumes that hung like a curtain in the cabin, but my father was undeterred. He would wish out loud for weekends of southerlies, calm seas and good fishing. He and his cobbers would head out to sea amply provisioned with meat pies, which they washed down with their home-brew or a keg of draft beer that Dad had brought home from Wellington. Invited occasionally to join them, I would try to adjust to the boat's motion, fumes and the digesting of meat pies, but the combination was often too much for my stomach. I would disgorge my lunch over the side and when the fish began to bite my father gave me the credit.

Butterfish, blue cod, snapper and grouper were plentiful. With buoys Dad often set out a long, 500-hook line. "We paid five shillings for a license and sold the fish for two bob each. Good money in those days," Dad later reminisced. Sometimes he would anchor the *Kia Ora* in Fisherman's Bay and other times in the Makara River right in front of our home. On a practical level Dad's fishing and hunting supplemented our diet and his sales from the game also improved the family's finances. During the shooting season, our garage would be festooned with unlucky wildlife, mostly ducks and black swans, from Lake Wairarapa. Dinner depended on the hunt. Mum made excellent hare and rabbit stews and prepared the swan and duck as tastily as in any hotel. "It's the Depression and we are living better than most," Dad would say. Because we had no refrigeration system—except the weather—Dad generously gave a lot of game away.

In those early years, together with the Monk brothers and Ted

Jarvis, Dad would go hunting around the coast past Te Kamara, which fronted on a beautiful bay. The coastal stretch was part of the Terawhiti sheep station, where Dad and his cobbers had use of a "rover's hut". It was all that was left of the large homestead and sheepshed that had burned down leaving only a large brick oven for baking bread. It was the sole shelter on this idyllic bay, which at that time was accessible only by boat or horse. Bales of wood had once been shipped from the bay to Wellington in a whale boat.

On one trip my Dad took me along. I was six years old and loved the excitement of the hunt, which was mostly for rabbits and hares but also brought down a few quail. The quail were lovely birds and I felt badly about their being killed. Ted Jarvis would cook up one hare stew after another and his culinary creations became our main diet during the hunt. There was a lot of laughter and joking at mealtime but one night Dad gave a cry of alarm when he looked into the stew prepared by Ted Jarvis to find two eyes staring back at him. In the chef's enthusiasm Ted had thrown in the hare's head for good measure.

Dad had no trouble talking his hunting mates into helping salvage the *Kia Ora*. Pat Carmody, an Irish-born jeweler from Wellington, and farmers Les Monk and Ted Jarvis joined in the memorable project, which quickly became the talk of Makara.

As soon as we Diederich offspring were old enough we followed old Tim Hurlihy up the hills. He carried a long muzzle-loading rifle which he called a blunderbuss, which indeed it was. Along with the gunpowder he would ram paper, tacks and ball bearings, pretty much anything he could find, down the muzzle. When he let fly at a hare or rabbit the gun would explode like a cannon. The first time I fired the ancient weapon its recoil knocked me backward, and for weeks I wore a black-and-blue shoulder bruise.

Both the rabbit and hare had been introduced into New Zealand by British colonists. The two little mammals (which are not identical) became the country's most serious pests, as well as the makings for stew at countless Depression-era dinner tables. Even though we dined on them, we children felt pity for the rabbits and hares in Makara, and were somewhat shocked to learn that in the South Island, Mum used to shoot rabbits from the car while Dad drove.

The rabbit plague played havoc with the nation's farmers for years. Mark Twain, visiting New Zealand in 1895, noted, "In New Zealand the rabbit plague began at Bluff [A town on the southern post point of the South Island]. The man who introduced the rabbit was banqueted and lauded; but they would hang him now if they could get him."

Nor were the fast-breeding bunnies the only worrisome wildlife. One Sunday while attending the Marist Brothers' school in Thorndon, a district of Wellington, I learned a lesson about whales. Dad, Uncle Brian and I had gone fishing in Uncle Brian's small row boat along the coast. We were in deep water when we suddenly spotted a big whale close by moving along between us and the coast. What was especially dangerous about this huge whale was the fact that she was frolicking with her calf, which was also breaking the surface. We were very close. My father signaled with his finger over his mouth to keep absolutely quiet and not attract the mother whale's attention. We sat there waiting. It seemed to take forever for the two animals to swim past us along the coast. How vulnerable we had been was soon demonstrated by later events.

The next morning a Marist school classmate broke the news: An Italian fisherman from Island Bay in a big boat had harpooned what was obviously our whale cow. She had reacted and, to save her calf, had flipped her two-ton baby out of the way with her tail. The calf had sailed through the air and landed on the fishing boat, smashing it and badly injuring the fisherman.

CHAPTER 11

Guerrilla Tactics

During the spring, when the apples were still green and sour, we youngsters turned into a guerrilla raiding party. Our leader was Desmond Hurlihy, 12 years old, and older than any of us Diederichs, who promised us that raiding orchards was not stealing but a healthy tradition to cull the apple and plum trees. Silently we shipped oars and slipped ashore, creeping through the grass into Art Hawkins' orchard. No one ever saw us, let alone caught us. Nor did anyone else really care but we didn't know it at the time.

Like military commandos we crawled under the trees and, with the aid of sticks, loosened the apples which dropped almost into our hands. We loved our apples green and we ate so many the result was a predictable upset stomach. "Greedy guts, guzzleguts!" my sisters Stellamaris and Quita would jibe, adding, "Serves you right. God is punishing you!" They would refuse to eat the purloined fruit.

However we guerrillas were convinced that it was also a sin to waste fruit. Art Hawkins and the other farmers had long since lost interest in their old orchards which had, like their dairy farms (because of competition from the bigger dairy farms elsewhere), begun to go into decline. Local farmers seldom bothered to gather the apples anymore allowing them to rot on the ground.

It was the same with peaches and plums. The farmers' wives were making fewer and fewer jams. My only concern was having to confess to raiding the orchards before Father Hurlihy. Penance usually consisted of reciting a dozen Hail Marys and the Stations of the Cross and even today while saying these prayers my mouth waters. Gooseberries and blackberries grew wild and we could crawl under the bushes and select the best. Nellie Hawkins had a front hedge of gooseberries and with her permission we gathered the biggest and juiciest for Mum to make delicious gooseberry pies.

For years it seemed I was always hungry at Makara. I later blamed my condition on the lean Depression years, but Dad took issue. It had nothing to do with the Depression, he corrected me: "It was because you had the appetite of a horse, I've never seen anyone who ate as much as you! "

Our breakfast was indeed a monstrous affair. I was usually first to the table in the early morning in order to be the first to pour the milk, which had a thick layer of cream, onto my porridge or Weetbix. "Mum, Berber has taken all the cream again," Quita would complain about my failure to stir the cream in with the milk. According to the guidelines propounded by today's food-police we ate all the wrong things: Sandwiches dripping with fat, golden syrup, bacon and sausages and eggs and even bread coated with sugar. But we were all lean.

Perhaps one reason was that we youngsters were so active. Our river, for example, was a world of its own. We had our favorite swimming spots, strategically located over what we knew were holes in the river bottom which allowed us to dive in from the bank and later from the swing bridge which was built across the river at Hawkins' place. When the tide was out, there were several fording places on the river, which was tidally influenced, where we could cross on foot. I would fetch the Hawkins' cows for milking and sure enough, as they left the paddocks and forded the river heading for the milkshed, they would plop, plop in the shallow water. But their manure was mostly masticated grass that soon dissolved in running water.

Another Makara Beach mystery came to light one night when Dad fell into the river. Several times a week Dad would remove the dunny can and bury the contents in a larger hole he had dug by the side of the river. As the hole was gradually filled with his buried treasure and he couldn't find a new place to dig, and forgetting his environmental concerns, he began to regularly toss the can's contents into our river. One night as he was emptying the receptacle he lost his footing and fell into the river along with the can. "I did it when the tide was going out, so it went off to sea," Dad confessed roaring with laughter in relating his ugly mishap and unexpected midnight swim.

But the tide was obviously not always going out. While swimming we found unexpected human proof to the contrary.

Dad did respect white-baiting season. There was no dumping when these transparent little fish that the Maoris called *inanga* began their run up the river. We could catch them in a fine white net near the ford at the Hawkins' where the water was shallow. Sometimes we caught them in front of our house. Mum made delicious whitebait fritters.

Eeling however was a slimy sport. We would fashion a pole from a large bamboo rod borrowed from the Hurlihys' place and tie a worm on a piece of string at the end of the pole. When the eel began eating the worm we would fling the black, slimy water creature onto the bank. The Hurlihys ate the eels—a British delicacy—but our family wouldn't touch them. During spring the Makara River became vibrant with life. Fluffy little ducklings and goslings sailed up and down behind their proud mothers. Even so our river was not always well-behaved. During a severe storm when the flooding was particularly bad, bloated carcasses of cattle and sheep would join the grotesque branches and trunks of trees being swept down to the sea.

Mushrooming season by contrast, was a gleeful time, not only because the delicate fungi, fried in butter, were a tasty treat, but also because gathering them was, for the family, a competitive sport. Racing over the hills we children would search out the little white buttons or the big umbrella-type varieties and try to be the first to fill our billy. At an early age we were taught the differences between an edible mushroom—described to us as manna from heaven—and a toadstool, denominated as the Devil's food from Hell. The Devil's food, usually tan in color, popped up in tempting profusion under the trees around the Hawkins' woolshed but we knew they were poisonous. As noted earlier, we became very possessive about Makara and we didn't like intruders, especially city people who came out mushrooming. But we couldn't do anything about their roaming over Hawkins' pastures. It was to all intents and purposes a free country.

Unlike mushrooming, collecting firewood, an early assignment and a tough one, was not at all fun. One cold winter day I was helping the Hurlihys cut and gather manuka wood. A driving hail-storm had forced us to take shelter under a manuka tree. Lovely Daphne Hurlihys was next to me, and her brothers, not waiting for the storm to ease, began bundling up the manuka firewood to drag down the hill. While they were occupied I confessed to Daphne that I intended to travel when I grew up, that suddenly I had decided there had to be more to the world than Makara and firewood. I was eight years old, Daphne the same age. My nose was running and I remember wiping it with the rough edge of the cuff of my old coat. A habit that hurt. She was noncommittal, which hurt even more. I then felt ashamed. It was the end of my first romance.

The Hurlihys were much poorer than most and it sounded as though, in my high-flown aspirations, I was bragging. I never forgot that unintended boast. Although in a way my declaration of determination at that moment drove me on, I didn't want to appear to be ashamed of friends because they were poor—least of all Daphne and her family.

As a youth I became acutely aware that New Zealand was still far from the egalitarian society that it aspired to be. The fact remained that, as everywhere, there were differences among people. Tim Hurlihy, Daphne's father, didn't seem to have any trace of the pioneer virtues of ambition and self-betterment that were supposed to be building this new country. Still, few people had work then and I suppose I should not have been critical of his working for the Council for a pittance mending the Makara road, shifting gravel from one side of the road to the other. A thankless job. The gravel would be flung out of the potholes when the milk truck, the baker's van, the fruit wagon, or other vehicles passed over them. But Tim refilled the potholes, year in and year out.

Poverty was looked upon with the Englishman's inherent fear of such a condition, and even asking for credit or personal borrowing was frowned upon as a practice of which to be ashamed.

Fortunately our family was spared the abject poverty that humbled so many previously prosperous people during the Depression. As in the unemployment-wracked cities, we had few luxuries. Yet life at Makara was full of offsetting pretenses. Brimming with daily adventure stories at Makara Beach, everyone wanted to talk and no one wanted to listen —it was an unfortunate family trait! We children could row our boat, play cowboys and Indians (yes, we had heard about them from America) on real horses, and otherwise enjoy our rugged fantasyland.

True to our colonialist ancestry, we grew up with imported heroes. It didn't occur to us to reenact our own country's Maori Wars or replay the valiant World War I acts of heroism by our Anzac relatives on the shores of Gallipoli. Rudyard Kipling hadn't sanctified them in his writings or poems.

CHAPTER 12

Makara's First Commuter

Farmers in the valley could tell the time by the telltale funnel of dust along Makara Road. It was Dad commuting by car to and from work in Wellington. Dad left home at 7 a.m. and returned at 8 o'clock at night. He was Makara's first regular commuter. When he decided the Gray's continental engine needed a rest he sold the workhorse automobile in 1929 and purchased a three-year-old Essex for 250 pounds. The Hudson-Essex agents advertised their vehicle as, "Wind outside, just fresh air inside."

Without a single mishap Dad was to drive that narrow winding road daily, except Sunday, for almost forty years. The road snaked down the narrow valley with a cliff on one side and the stream on the other. There was no room to maneuver but in those days ours was often the only car on that road. Encroaching cows and sheep were quick to scatter as Dad approached. Mum didn't drive but she was queen of backseat drivers and upset us with her continuous cautions to Dad:"Now Bern, slow down, watch out. That was near!"

Good naturedly Dad would laugh. Years later I asked him how he put up with Mum's incessant backseat-driving. "I loved her," he said.

This commuting engendered neighborliness between Dad and the farmers. He gave those who needed a ride (there was no public transport) lifts to and from town and in turn they generously shared their cloudy home brew beer.

Tim Hurlihy and for a time Art Hawkins who had run off to sea in a sailing vessel in his youth were roadmen. They would rest on their shovels or ignore their boiling billy to wave to Dad. It all became ritualistic and even the cows lifted their heads and seemed to salute Dad as he passed.

At home Mum was overwhelmed with domestic chores. Daily she washed, starched and ironed Dad's shirt invariably having to dry it in winter, along with his underwear and socks, before the open fire in the living room. Our winter's sun wouldn't dry a hand-kerchief. Dad always wore a coat and tie to work. Clean-shaven, he looked young, smart and athletic. He was an early health nut and had his medicinal fads. At one time he believed mineral oil was very good for what he called "the system," and we all had to con-sume great quantities of mineral oil which at least was better than the cure-all castor oil, or prunes.

The "dehumanized place," Dad called the city and his warn-ings about pedophiles made us share his bias. By the beginning of the 1930s our capital city of Wellington, which grew up during the nineteenth-century days of mass immigration, still had a few dingy, crowded slums left and poverty was no stranger in this land "of milk and honey."

Dad would point out the Te Aro slums, truly Dickensian, on our rare visits to the city, stressing that their unsanitary living conditions produced disease and even epidemics. "How lucky you are to live at Makara!" he would exult.

In fact the city even in the 1930s had a rather strong country air. Horses were everywhere and their manure left a pungent barn-yard odor along Wellington's best shopping streets. Far from both-ering me, horses were one of my first loves. There was still a water trough for horses before Barrett's Pub on Lambton Quay. The trough quenched the thirst of the impressive teams of full-blooded draft horses that slowly clopped through Wellington hauling bar-rels of beer to the city's many pubs. Tram drivers clanged their bells incessantly to hurry the big Clydesdale draft horses off the tram tracks. The Gear Company's single-horse meat wagon was a particularly agile vehicle as it emerged onto Lambton Quay oppo-site yet another pub. However, horse-drawn Hansom cabs had all but disappeared.

While Father was a genuine nature-lover his anti-city bias was also due in part to economics. City rents were excessively high and accommodations were at a premium; moreover the latter did not offer the kind of home he wanted for us children. The irony was that his German-born father, Bernard Joseph Diederich, had made and then lost a fortune in Wellington real estate at the end of the nineteenth century.

Both our parents were very proud people. In fact Mum acted at times like a misplaced aristocrat. She was obsessed with table manners, elocution, etiquette and family values. (Only once did I recall her getting her Irish up. It was at the table and she fired off a banger [sausage] on a fork at Dad for what reason I don't recall. Dad ducked just in time. The missile flew over his head and imbedded itself in the wallpaper, dripping gravy. It remained stuck on the wall all day like a piece of unappetizing avant-garde art.) However it wasn't all class-consciousness or snobbery with Mum, as it was her firm belief that to get anywhere in the world that we were entering, you had to be well equipped, with the best education and English manners. She had decided that we would one day be mingling with the world's best. Values, moral character and conduct were extremely important to her. Even more important of course was religion. Yet after saying grace, Mum would issue orders: "Hold your knife and fork properly! This is how you use your soup spoon," and she would demonstrate sweeping the spoon away.

Paradoxically Mum was politically on the left and voted Labor. She had some Labor cabinet minister friends and leaned to socialism. Dad voted Nationalist and believed in capitalism but was far too generous a person ever to become a real capitalist himself. He also championed the underdog and would damn "scabs" (workers who break a union picket line) to "Hell's fire." Being a scab in New Zealand, at least in those days, could mean total rejection by fellow workers.

The country was painfully young and was still in search of its vision as an egalitarian society. And we continued to believe in God as destiny. Any misfortune was an act of God.

As the Depression took firmer hold, workmen suddenly appeared with picks and shovels and began digging into the hillside to widen the Karori side of Makara Hill road. They were, my father explained to us, bank managers and other professionals who had lost their jobs because of the Depression and were now being given a chance to work, with picks and shovels, for the state. Whether in fact there were that many unemployed bankers I doubted, but Dad made a point.

Yet, in spite of the tough times, in our family the idea of asking for credit was *tapu* and looked down upon as an evil akin to stealing, at least on the surface. In New Zealand society generally, credit carried such a stigma that no respectable person would admit to resorting to borrowing, or buying on the installment plan. Doing either was something to hide something more like a "social disease" (as venereal infections were called in those days). An upstanding person simply didn't ask for credit. It was a cash-and-carry life, far from today's credit-card, cashless society.

So it was something of a shock when I learned that the trips to an office at the bottom of Plimmer Steps in Wellington with a small brown envelope were for monthly payments to a credit union. Mum had been secretly purchasing our school clothes through a credit union, a forerunner of the credit card. It also took years for Dad and Mum to pay off the mortgage on our Makara house. For all the bias against credit, in those days Charles Dickens' books about social inequities and human greed were very much on people's minds. I had at first become a Dickensian fan by osmosis. I can't recall then reading about Little Nell of The Old Curiosity Shop and that mean bugger Quilp, but I knew all about them and was happy to be at Makara and away from the mean-spirited city life portrayed by Dickens in the 19th century.

Family Album

During the winter of 1929 older sister Quita and the author, as little brother, take cover from the winter in our parent's bed at Makara Beach.

Our growing brood poses for Dad on the Makara
front lawn.

The solitary white rock on the beach was as smooth as
marble and became our favorite perch.

Glorious summer on Makara Beach. Our private wonderland was also our sandbox.

Grandmother, "Nana" Margaret McCarthy McCleary,
Mum's Mum, with her hands full of Diederich children.
Born in County Cork Ireland,Nana came to New
Zealand as a child . She married Grandpa, James
McCleary, who was a first generation New Zealander,
born in Auckland.

Grandpa McCleary kept an eye on us. Stellamaris poses
for the camera at left.

The Makara school house.

Makara crossroads. St. Mattias Anglican church with the
War Memorial in the foreground.

Incredible excitement we get to see and examine our first
aeroplane when the pilot makes a forced landing in
Hawkin's cow paddock across the river. The pilot escaped
injury. We took awed if temporary possession.

Every man woman and child was a hunter and fisherman.
We hunted the vermin introduced into the country by
immigrants: mostly rabbits, hares and quail. At aged six the
author accompanied Dad and his Makara farmer pals on a
weeklong hunt in the hills above Te Kamara. In the pictures
are Les Monk and Ted Jarvis and the day trophies.

Amid diesel fumes and the aroma of meat pieces out launch
Kai Ora leaves its anchorage in the river before our house
heading for the open sea. It was good fishing in those days.
Plenty of Blue Cod and delicious butterfish.

Growing up on the beach with Dad on the left and our
venerable old Essex automobile in the background.

Our horse Ginger.

Cadet's chosen to represent St. Pat's College in early 1942
at a military training program preparing for war. The
camp was on the outskirts of the town of Dannevirke,
100 miles north of Wellington.

The 1940 Centennial Eucharistic Congress
celebrated on the ground of St. Pat's College, Wellington.

Makara Beach on a calm day.

In keeping with the family's rugby tradition the author as
a member of St. Pat's College First Fifteen in 1942.

Cousin Father Des Scanlon poses against the new bathhouse at Makara beach in 1940 before returning to Guadalcanal in the Solomon Islands. From left to right, a young friend, Stellamaris, Father Des, Quita, Tony and Brian.

The Sunday crowd on our Makara tennis court that Dad built.

Our personal trainer Uncle Brian (McCleary). On his
return from Germany at the end of the First World War,
during which he served in France and later Germany as
an ambulance driver, he became Australasia boxing
champion. In 1924 he was a member of that year's
famous All Blacks rugby team.

Best Wishes
From
Stella

Mum and Dad. Stella and Bernie.

Bernard Joseph Diederich, painting in oils a scene of the
Milford Sound after a bicycle trip down the South Island.

During the roaring '20s in Christchurch Dad, Mum,
Uncle Brian and sisters Auntie Hilda and Madge had a
wonderful time.

The Culverden hotel, an old stagecoach stop before
crossing New Zealand's Southern Alps. In 1923 it was a
great enterprise for Dad and Uncle Brian. They took over
the hotel, which permitted them plenty of time to
continue their rugby playing.

The Scanlon store in Charleston, New Zealand, in 1868
when it was a booming gold town. Great-grandmother
Maria Hurly Scanlon is holding her latest child in front of
the store. The old town vanished with the gold.

Our goldminer great-grandfather Patrick Scanlon, who
fled Ireland to California, Australia and finally New
Zealand in the 1860s. Seen here on holiday in Sydney,
Australia, posing with son Jack's wife, May, and their two
boys. The couple also had a baby girl, Nora.

The McCleary clan. Left to right: Our mother Stella,
Auntie Hilda, Nana, Madge, Brian and Jim, Grandpa
and Auntie Doris. The family portrait was taken in
Dunedin.

Our military ancestor John McCleary had this two-story house built at 23
Alten Road, Auckland in the 1850s. This is where Grandpa McCleary his six
brothers and a sister grew up.

Maria Hurly Scanlon with her youngest son Jack. She was
about 42 years of age when this portrait was taken.

The Diederich family traveling from their farm in the
Wairarpa Valley to town in the big dray. Great-grandmother Muta is seated at the back to make sure none of
the children falls off or is left behind.

Grandpa Bernard Joseph Diederich, with his parents and
family, at his new home on Waterloo Street in the Lower
Hutt.

Born in Germany in 1858, Johann was the eldest
Diederich boy to come to New Zealand and the first to
marry. He then went off to Madras, India, with his wife.
As a sergeant in the Madras Volunteers he is at the
extreme right. The family left India in 1908 to settle in
Western Australia.

The 4-masted barque *Pamir* on which the author served
during WWII sailing across the Pacific between
Wellington and San Francisco twice.

Aboard the *Pamir* the author (left) and shipmates calm
down an Albatross, mindful of the ancient mariner's curse.

The armed American tanker, *Port Republic*, in Persia (now
Iran) taking on a load of fuel for warships in the Pacific
Theater of World War II . This was the second, U.S.-flag
T-2 tanker on which the author served.

Sister Stellamaris at St Mary's College in Wellington.

CHAPTER 13

Picnics & Dixieland

The framed photographs that eventually went up on the walls of our Makara home told of an earlier chapter of the Diederich family saga. It centered around rugby. Rugby was an important part of our family tradition and one didn't joke about what was also our national sport. (Years later at the Marist Brothers school where soccer instead of rugby was played, I barely missed making the New Zealand national soccer team. I tried out and came close to being one the chosen eleven. Even so, the family was not upset that I was not representing our country's top team in "that game.") There were a lot of photos of Dad in official portraits of the various teams on which he had played, occupying the place of honor as the handsome, lean, young captain and wing forward. He had captained the Manawatu and Canterbury teams, and was at one time New Zealand's youngest representative team player.

Having been born into a rugby-mad family meant that I was expected to thoroughly enjoy being taken to Wellington's Central Park in winter to watch an important rugby match. Instead I would have preferred to stay at Makara fishing in the river. Seated on bare benches in the open-air park with an icy wind blowing was not what I considered great fun. But later, attending St. Patrick's College in Wellington, each of us boys, in turn, made the college First Fifteen rugby team.

Scholastic achievement was important, especially for my sisters, but our parents felt that for us boys, excelling at sports was equally if not more crucial. If we hadn't made the top rugby team and scored a few goals we would have failed both our parents. (In fairness, my sisters, Stellamaris and Quita, did excel at tennis.)

As it had been with Mum's mother, it was rugby that had brought Mum and her chosen one—Dad—together and led them down the aisle to holy matrimony. Hence rugby was to be our secular guiding light. It did not take the place of our God but it occupied a position usually reserved for the highest of deities. And indeed we had a lot to thank rugby for.

By contrast with Mum's forebears, on my father's side of the family there was no previous rugby tradition, the Diederichs' having immigrated from a soccer-playing country. Diederich rugby began with my father himself and his brother, Uncle Roy; the latter became captain of Wellington's Victoria University First Fifteen, who toured Australia and in all played 40 first-class representative matches.

My father likewise excelled at the sport. He continued to compete in it after leaving school, an adult avocation which was fashionable then and still is. Like his German-born father, Dad also had a natural talent for drawing. He could sketch anything. Yet he declined to make the teaching of art a career, even though he was assured of such a position at Palmerston North High School. Instead Dad left secondary school at eighteen to work on his family's farm.

Dad enjoyed drawing caricatures of the current rugby stars and the renditions were so good that they won Dad a job offer from a magazine as a cartoonist, which he turned down.

Having been born in 1899, Dad (baptized Bernard John) used to say, "The Boer War started the day I was born and Queen Victoria was on the throne." He was to live under six monarchs.

Dad's place of birth was the Diederich family quarters above his father's shop and cabinet-making factory on Cuba Street, one of Wellington's main thoroughfares. Dad was the first son and was named Bernard after his father. (Siblings Girlie and Tom were born next but both died as babies of diphtheria before they were a year old.) Winnie was next, followed by Frank who was born at the new house Grandpa had built in 1906 on Waterloo Road at Lower

Hutt. It was a big house with excellent stables for the coach horses and they also had a maid.

Uncle Roy Diederich was also born there. It's hard to have favorite uncles as I loved them all, but Uncle Roy was special. I enjoyed watching him play rugby at university and later, after he became a distinguished lawyer, even attended court to watch his legal skills. After he became assistant attorney general of the Fiji Islands in 1938 (Fiji was then under British rule), in his spare time he coached a Fijian rugby team to victory.

A deeply spiritual man, Uncle Roy refused an officer's commission in the army during World War II and instead volunteered to fight the Axis as a private. He was killed in Italy while crossing the River Po during a German mortar barrage a fortnight before the war ended.

Elvie, Geoff, Nonie and Molly followed Roy into the world. Along with the seven children there was Grandpa Diederich's German-born mother, Gertrude, whom they called Muta. She was a large, robust woman who spoke little English and was an accomplished gardener. Muta passed away in 1909. The family continued to live in Lower Hutt until 1912, when Grandpa Diederich decided it would be ideal for the children to grow up on a farm. He found 300 acres of excellent farmland at Raumai in the Pohangana Valley near the Totara Reserve, seventeen miles from Palmerston North.

It was good, flat river land. The Diederichs' house became the local post office.

But for all his expertise as a furniture-maker Grandpa Diederich was too trusting to be a good businessman. Dad told us that a certain lawyer "diddled father out of the farm." Having lost his farm Grandpa went back to the furniture business in Palmerston North in 1913.

In 1922 the family persuaded Dad to enter the police college in Wellington. After graduation he was assigned to Christchurch where he ended up in the detective branch. His maternal Uncle Jerry Scanlon was instrumental in Dad's joining the police force.

Uncle Jerry, who had traveled with his mother from Ireland to

the gold fields of New Zealand to join his father, had been governor of the old Terrace Jail in Wellington and, later the prison at
Lyttelton. Family lore credited Jerry Scanlon with having insti-
tuted a number of modern-day prison reforms, among them per-
mitting convicts to serve time working on farms with only their
honor as chains.

While serving in the police force Dad continued playing rugby
in his free time, which had its practical uses. One day in
Christchurch he used a rugby tackle to catch a thief who was running from the crime scene. Dad overtook the man and brought
him down with a flying tackle and a thud on the hard city pave-
ment.

Yet Dad rarely mentioned to us his life as a policeman or why
he had not made a career of it. He had friends who rose to high
positions on the force and one had become a police commissioner.
However there were some clues to Dad's reticence.

A young second cousin whose father was a policeman in the
South Island told me that my father had had a donnybrook with a
superior who wanted to falsify a report and thereby denigrate a
Catholic nun who had accidentally drowned in a tidal river. A
visiting fire-and-brimstone preacher was leading a Church of England crusade against New Zealand Catholics at the time, and
Dad's police superior was cooperating in the campaign. He allegedly wanted to rule the nun's death a suicide, claiming she was
pregnant. As an Irish-German loyal Catholic, my father, according
to the story from this cousin's family, punched his superior in the
nose and then handed in his resignation.

For his part Dad said there was indeed a great deal of antago-
nism in the civil service and police between Catholics and Protestants during that period but that the story was not true. Dad's
explanation for not continuing his career in law enforcement was
that he couldn't see any future with the police, so he quit and he
and my maternal Uncle Brian joined forces to become hotelkeepers.

It was on the rugby field in Christchurch that Dad had met
Brian McCleary, who was already a well-known footballer and boxer.
Brian had only recently returned from World War I in France and

Germany. He had boxed in France, won the heavyweight title there, and on his return become New Zealand heavyweight boxing champion. One of Brian's younger sisters, Stella, another rugby faithful, attended the matches which saw Dad and Brian playing on the same side. She was impressed by the young man playing wing forward—he was fast. "What's his name? Diederich? What kind of name is that? Is he Catholic?" she asked.

The inquisitive young lady, who was to become our mother, was a trained nurse and, like many of her male friends in Dunedin, in the South Island where she was born and brought up, she possessed the education and ability to become a doctor. But despite the fact that New Zealand was among the first countries to give women the vote, in 1891, they were not encouraged to become physicians, only nurses.

Life was full of fun for Stella and her new rugby-playing beau. It was the rip-roaring 1920s, even in isolated New Zealand, and the roar was never louder than during a glorious rugby match. It was after the roar died down a bit following one match that my father proposed, capping a whirlwind courtship, and they were married in Christchurch on Oct. 31, 1922. Mum was 21 years of age and Dad had just turned 23. Stellamaris was born on April 6, 1924, and Quita was to follow on June 11, 1925, and I on July 18, 1926.

Besides her brother Brian and another brother, James, my mother had three sisters. As I have mentioned each of them had been married to men who returned from World War I shattered physically and mentally. Aunty Doris' husband, for instance, had fought in the trenches in France and been wounded. A German soldier had fired a *coup de grace*, with a pistol, that blew a hole in my Uncle's head. Miraculously he survived but wore a metal plate in his head. None of the sisters' postwar marriages lasted.

Our family photo albums were filled with snapshots of Father and Mother in formal evening attire attending one party after another, posing for their pictures respectively in dinner suits and chic dresses of the time. There were poses of them during dances at the Dixieland ballroom in Christchurch, and with their friends and relatives on picnic spreads beside their prized automobiles. My father was an amateur photographer and a good one. He could set the delayed exposure and get into the picture. He and his fellow rugby players enjoyed themselves famously in spite of the country's orthodox Victorian morality and strong Church of England bias.

It was in Culverton in 1923 where Dad and Uncle Brian were playing rugby that they decided to become hotel partners. Together they bought the license to the popular Culverton Hotel and pub in North Canterbury that had originated as a stagecoach stop on the route through the Lewis Pass to the West Coast. Dad quit the police force. The Hotel-pub was a good distance from Christchurch where both of my elder sisters were born. The laws concerning alcohol were extraordinarily strict and the sale of beer and liquor was prohibited after 6 p.m. even in that quiet farming community.

A local police constable, according to my father, was not an honest cop. In fact Dad referred to the constable as a "rottin' soul," and charged that the man had lowered the boom on Dad and Uncle Brian in their first year as publicans.

"Of course we were serving some farmers after hours, my father explained in telling the story years later. "You couldn't shut them out at 6 p.m. no matter how you tried in those days. No honorable publican would turn his back on a thirsty farmer,"

The local constable on the beat actually wanted the pub for himself, Dad charged, and set up a conspiracy.

"He got a fellow to accuse us of selling spirits after hours and we lost our license," Dad said. In fact neither Dad or Uncle Brian were on the job at the time but out of the province playing rugby. Once you had your hotel-pub license revoked, it was impossible to get another. (The old Culverton hotel was destroyed by fire in 1949. A worker removing old lead paint with a blowtorch set the building on fire and it took just an hour to be turned into ashes. Today there is a portrait of Uncle Brian in his Allblack rugby jersey peers down on the bar of the new hotel from the wall.)

Unable to operate his own establishment, Dad decided to help run other people's hotels. He worked at the Empire Hotel in Christchurch while seeking a more promising job. But hard times had come to New Zealand. Jobs were becoming more difficult to find, and unemployment was high. The good times had to come to an end as the Great Depression found its way to far-off New Zealand. There was no escaping this economic calamity. No country was immune.

CHAPTER 14

The Royal Tiger

It was years later that I learned from Dad the real reason for our move to Wellington from Christchurch, that most English of New Zealand cities where I was been born at 9 Suffolk Street, Linwood, a residential section. The house with some modifications still stands at the end of the short street not far from the Provincial Pub on Cashel St.

The move to Wellington came shortly after Dad and Uncle Brian had lost their license to operate their Culverton hotel-pub. A friend, Jack Murphy, invited Dad to Wellington to work at the "Old Identities," an ineffably named pub on Manner Street at the bottom of Boulcott Street where the St. George Hotel stands today. And so we moved. Some of the most important city fathers had their faces carved in wood on the facade of the Old Identities.

Shortly afterward Dad received an even better offer, to manage Wellington's Royal Tiger Hotel-pub. He accepted. It proved to be a wise decision. He was to remain there for fifteen years. Two years after he took the position, by the end of 1931, New Zealand was feeling the full weight of the worldwide economic depression. That December there were hunger riots in Dunedin, Mum's birthplace.

Much later in life, a friend of our father said that "Bernie"— Dad—was a born psychiatrist "who could manage a bar, pump beer and measure whiskey while all the time listening to his patients-customers." The main topic was naturally rugby. However this friend insisted that during the Depression, Dad had dissuaded more than one man from jumping to his death off the new Kelburn viaduct that replaced the old wooden one in 1931. (It was as if they had completed the new viaduct in time for a whole series of Depression-related suicides.)

Dad spoke of the Damon Runyonesque characters who frequented the Tiger which was located in what was then the toughest section of Wellington. Nearby Haining Street passed for the capital's Chinatown, even though it was a short street and only a few families lived there. The Chinese of Haining Street ran illegal Pakapoo gambling dens. They were accused by some of the prohibitionist groups of also operating opium dens.

Dad's pub got its name from the British army's Royal Bengal Tigers brigade who had been garrisoned nearby on Taranaki Street early in the colony. During his years at the Royal Tiger, Dad witnessed a great deal of history firsthand, since the old wooden structure was also just around the corner from New Zealand Army Headquarters on Buckle Street. (When I tried unsuccessfully to enlist in the army upon the outbreak of war in 1939, the recruiting sergeant at Buckle Street called my father. "Your son is big for eighteen," he told Dad. "Like bloody hell!" Dad replied. "He is thirteen.")

During a violent strike in Wellington in 1913, every window of the Royal Tiger Hotel had been shattered by strikers because the Special Constables, the government's strikebreakers, had dropped in for a pint or two. Theirs was thirst-engendering and hateful work. Dad said that if he had been there then they wouldn't have been served. Among Dad's regular customers were a few spit-and-polish soldiers who still believed that the empire was held together with military Sam Brown belts, beneath which beat the proud hearts of the Imperial Army.

Four years after Dad began work at the Royal Tiger there was another threat. As a protest by unemployed workers broke up before Parliament, some rioted, smashing windows down Lambton Quay and Willis Street. They didn't reach the Tiger however, which this time escaped undamaged. Even if they had, Dad would probably have controlled the situation. He could do that sort of thing.

As a neighborhood fixture, the pub was as much an institution and center of male social life in New Zealand as it was in

England, Ireland, Scotland and Wales. Yet Dad rarely talked of his work. There were numerous reasons. It was honest labor. But the country was divided in those days between the glorious pub with its booze, and the strong prohibitionist movement, members of which in New Zealand were called "Wowsers," which rhymed with "bowser"—the name of the original petrol pump. The "Wowsers" enforced public abstinence after 6 p.m., and, if they had had their way, every pub in New Zealand would have been shut down and converted into an evangelical center of worship.

We youngsters were never invited to the Tiger. A pub was no place for children, Dad explained. "When you go to school, they are going to ask you, 'What does your father do?' Tell them, 'He is a salesman,'" Dad once said, adding, "and I am." It was the custom, even though New Zealand aspired to be a classless society, for children, and even adults, to ask, "What does your father do?" It established a person's position in society. There were still private hotels that were not licensed to sell alcohol; thus Dad could be on safe ground. Dad was a salesman and to friends I could add, he runs a hotel (without specifying whether it was pub-less.)

With pubs forced to close at 6 p.m., and most offices closing at five o'clock in the afternoon, more beer was consumed in pubs during that intervening hour than during the entire day. It was referred to as the "six o'clock swill". Customers drained handle after handle, as the big glass mugs were called, with one eye on the clock. The pub began as an exclusively male institution but women were later permitted to enter so-called "private" bars, away from the "public" bar which remained a male preserve.

The Royal Tiger provided Dad good contacts that resulted in fringe benefits. He would bring home a huge coal sack of Bluff oysters—40 dozen—for one New Zealand pound. During the hunting season he would bring home a kit of ten to 20 mutton birds from the South Island. They were plump, petite birds laden with fat and they required a lot of cooking. A ship's captain brought Dad alligator pears which we later learned were also called avocados. Dad often brought home exotic little souvenirs from the Cook Islands or Fiji that had been presented to him.

One customer bestowed on Dad a pregnant Pomeranian. It was a delicate dog but she produced five fluffy pups that won our family's heart. Geoffrey loved them too much and accidentally suffocated two of them. (It was not long afterward that a black cocker spaniel followed me home and we adopted him too and named him Astor. Wise enough not to endanger his welcome, Astor was careful not to chase the local sheep.) Another time someone gave Dad a huge Angora rabbit. When it began devouring Grandpa's vegetable garden next door we exiled the rabbit, much like Napoleon, to our island in the river only to discover that the rodent could swim. We watched in astonishment as it swam back to rejoin our family. The big rabbit was then given away.

In a reciprocal gesture of generosity, on Monday mornings Dad would often take fresh fish he had caught on Sunday as gifts to some of his loyal customers. He became an equally popular figure in Makara; not the least of the reasons was that when he was in a hospitable mood, which was most of the time, he would bring home a five-gallon wooden keg of beer which he would open in the garage for thirsty local fishermen, farmers and other friends.

It often seemed that Dad had all the fun and that the moves to Wellington and later Makara had affected Mum the most. She had left her girlhood friends behind in the South Island and talked nostalgically of her school days at one of the Catholic schools in Dunedin, and of the lovely places her mother had at New Brighton beach and at Waitaki.

CHAPTER 15

"Big Black Jim"

Festive entertainment at Makara was a singsong at someone's home. An accordion, banjo, guitar, mouth organ or piano were the popular musical instruments. The Saturday night parties would rotate around the valley. The men drank home brew (beer) and talked rugby and horses while the women served sandwiches, sipped tea or a spot of sherry and gossiped. Beer was not a lady's drink, unless it was part of a "shandy," a mixture of beer and lemonade served in a small glass.

Even children were permitted to attend the monthly Saturday night dance at the Makara Hall. Our Hall, like those all over rural New Zealand, was the heart of community life. Its simple wooden structure was as old as the area's first settlement. There was a nominal entrance fee on dance night to help pay the musicians, if they required payment. (Not all did.) Everyone dressed in their best. Men wore coats and ties and women were resplendent in party dress. No alcoholic beverages were permitted in the Hall and the men folk, except if they were courting and could overcome their shyness enough to ask their ladies to dance, spent their time outside next to their cars drinking beer.

Young ladies sometimes had to dance with each other because most of the men preferred talking and drinking with their mates to dancing. There was no policeman at Makara and I never saw one anywhere in the community the whole time we lived there.

During World War II, Mum was one of the chief organizers and fund-raisers for the farewell for each of our young men going off to fight the Germans or Japanese. As a going-away present, the departing soldier, airman or sailor received a handsome watch engraved with his name. Our neighbor Jack Neilson, Scandy's eldest son who worked on the family farm and whom we all liked, was one of the first to get a "send-off," as they called the dance that accompanied the presentation. A cuppa (tea), sandwiches and cake would be served during the evening, and there was always a raffle of a lamb or two contributed by a farmer to help defray the cost of the watch and the send-off. Jack Neilson didn't return from the War. He was killed in the North Africa campaign.

Practical jokes were always big with my father. He loved to play them and had a great sense of the ridiculous. At the Royal Tiger, he recalled, there was always time for laughter amid the barroom hubbub. Although his customers, he liked to say, were not exactly Wellington high society, they were rich in spirit, at least after hoisting a few at the Tiger. Dad didn't have a prejudiced bone in his body. He judged a man on his ability, not his color. One of his friends was one of the few black persons in Wellington at the time, a huge man named Jim Martin.

A West Indian, from the island of Barbados, Jim Martin was a good amateur singer and showman. He had a deep voice and, we kids believed, was as accomplished a vocalist as the then-famous American bass singer, Paul Robeson. Jim Martin had lived in the United States, toiled on ships, and finally came ashore in Wellington, taking on work on the wharf.

The first time my father brought Mr. Martin home to Makara for a weekend to go fishing, for us kids it was Christmas and Guy Fawkes Day put together. When Mr. Martin (as we called him) rolled out of bed we couldn't believe his color. He was black, blacker than any man we had ever seen. (We had literally never seen a black person before.) He had his own banjo and sang to us a repertoire of songs, among them one entitled *All Birds Look Like a Chicken to Me*. He was the star of several Saturday night parties at Tim Hurlihy's and Mary Jarvis's.

Peeping into the guestroom the morning after his arrival at our place we marveled at Mr. Martin's blackness against the white

sheets. As he got to know us he told us about the world. We came
to love him but felt his stories were too outlandish to be true. We
believed he must be fibbing when he said that black men like
himself couldn't walk on the sidewalk with white men in some
towns in America.

In Wellington Mr. Martin lived near the illegal Pakapoo gambling dens that were located on Haining Street in the vicinity of
the Royal Tiger. The insular "Wowsers" were always spreading tales
about the Chinese who lived in this tiny exotic corner of
Wellington. They considered it a dangerous ghetto and said the
Chinese had strange customs. New Zealand was such an ingrown
place, this small center of foreign culture in the capital was seen as
potentially dangerous.

Dad related one story crying with laughter, illustrating just
how exotic the small Chinese neighborhood could become. It was
Guy Fawkes Day and "Big Jim," as Jim Martin was known in
town, dropped by Sam the Chinaman's butcher shop which was
also a Pakapoo (gambling) "bank."

"Sam, could I look at the latest bank?" Big Jim asked. Sam sat
down and showed him the numbers. Jim surreptitiously put his
cigar down between his knees and lit the fuse on a huge firecracker,
slipping it under Sam's chair. Big Jim thanked Sam and left.

Everyone in the neighborhood heard the explosion. When Sam
recovered from the shock, he ran wildly down Taranaki Street in
search of Big Jim with a huge meat cleaver poised for action.

Everyone got into the act. Local characters who played the
bank went to Sam the Chinaman who was still holding his heart
hours later and reported: "Big Jim is coming back." Sam spent the
rest of the day lying in wait with his meat cleaver. Despite Sam's
state of preparedness Big Jim managed that very same day to put a
double banger—firecracker—under Sam the Chinaman's feet. Jim
arranged for a friend to distract Sam while he tossed the firecracker
from the opposite direction. The whole of seedy Haining Street
and Upper Taranaki street was in an uproar.

Another time Dad was bringing Big Jim home to our place in
Makara. "It was a terribly dark night and we gave this lady a lift.

She got in the back and got the shock of her life. She had sat on Jim's lap. She hadn't seen him in the dark because his eyes were closed and he was fast asleep."

Jim was a big man, six feet three inches tall, wide-shouldered and powerful. He worked on the Wellington wharf for many years and lived in Martin Square, which he liked to say was named after him. In fact it was named after a New Zealand farmer, Johnny Martin, of the Wairarapa Valley who had established the town of Martinborough which became Mum and Dad's home in later life.

CHAPTER 16

Anzac Day

Each April 25th, the most solemn and seemingly coldest day of the year, I would join Uncle Brian and several of his former army comrades to attend the dawn parade before the Wellington Cenotaph war memorial. It was Anzac Day, the day both New Zealanders and Australians remember their countrymen who died in World War I especially at Gallipoli. That day patriotism stood tall in both Australia and New Zealand. It was also the day that our country with little more than one million in population didn't realize that the blood she had shed for empire was far too excessive and not necessarily in the interest of New Zealand. The letters Anzac stood for Australian, New Zealand Army Corps and both nations, part of the British empire, were extremely proud of their sacrifices.

It was usually under harsh Wellington skies when we arrived in the Nash from Makara long before dawn broke.

The parade should have taught me as a child the horrors of war, but it didn't. It had the reverse effect. True, there were survivors with empty arm sleeves and other telltale mementos of that terrible war. These scarred men, many of whom had fought in the trenches in France after surviving Gallipoli, would march proudly behind the bagpipes and bugle bands. The martial music would energize them and, following the ceremony at the Cenotaph, they would march through Wellington with shoulders back and heads held high. Those lucky enough to have returned with their right arms intact would swing them giving snappy salutes and eyes right. These survivors proudly displayed, on their tweed jackets and dark wool suit coats, breasts bedecked with large silver medals and ribbons. The ceremonies seemed to make them whole again even though their mental and physical souvenirs of history's most crippling war to that point were still fresh in their memory. Also present were a few surviving veterans of New Zealand's first overseas war in South Africa against the Boers.

I would keep up with the heroes by running alongside, and I knew that one day I would, like them, be called to our patriotic duty to defend the empire. It was an uncomplicated imperial world and we boasted that most of it belonged to us, as members of the British Empire on which the sun never set. What we didn't know then was that classic imperialism would soon be swept away by a second world conflagration.

Everyone, including civilian onlookers, had a red paper poppy that had been sold to collect money for the old and needy soldiers. The slogan was: "We shall remember them." The worst-case Veterans were those who had returned shell-shocked or as victims of poison gas.

Poi Theabold, a friend of Uncle Brian, was a veteran of Gallipoli. He came to live at Grandpa's place for a while during the Depression until he got a job. I listened to his first hand accounts of fighting the Turks. Most of our Veterans of Gallipoli didn't blame the young Winston Churchill, First Lord of the Admiralty, who had enthusiastically embraced the planned campaign to land on the Turkish peninsula and seize Constantinople (now Istanbul) to relieve the pressure on Russia, then an ally. (Turkey had joined Germany and Austria in World War I against the Allies, including Russia.)

Soldiers blamed poor leadership in carrying out the campaign which lasted nine months and in which nearly a quarter of a million men lost their lives on the side of the Anzacs, British and French. The Turks suffered roughly the same number of casualties. The only well-organized part of the campaign, the Anzac veterans used to say, was the ultimate secret evacuation of all the surviving allied troops, in an operation that fooled the Turks and didn't cost a life.

The description by many ex-soldiers of Anzac Cove and its steep cliff in Turkey, so far away, seemed to fit the description of Makara Beach. Strangely, other Gallipoli veterans seldom talked of the pain and the misery of the war. To all of us these veterans were heroes.

Unlike the professional soldiers of Europe with their long tradition of fighting wars, the Anzacs for the most part were sheep farmers and other civilians who were much more free-spirited and independent. In the end they made much better soldiers to fight such a campaign as Gallipoli, which called for a great deal of personal initiative in order to fight and survive. Like rabbits they burrowed into the face of cliffs. Moreover the former farmhands and day laborers could call on their physical strength to fight the Turks in hand-to—hand combat. With trenches so close they often exchanged gifts with "Johnny Turk" and used blood—curdling cries of in broken Arabic, learned in the dives of Cairo, when they attacked. In the summer months the Anzac uniform was shorts and boots. The sight of these bronzed half naked men was a shock to the spit-and-polish British officers. The Anzacs, too, were proud that they had faced the best commander in the Turkish army, Lieut. Col. Mustafa Kemal. As one veteran friend of Uncle Brian used to say, "We got Kemal his job." Kemal, later known as Ataturk, went on to become the modernizer of his country.

World War I was the only subject in which I was disappointed with my father. Because he was too young, Dad had not gone to the war. I felt he should have signed up despite his youth. Dad would sigh when he saw what the war had done to these men, and never tired of repeating, "Man's inhumanity to man makes count-less thousands mourn."

One member of the Diederich side of our family did serve and was killed at Gallipoli. He was Claude Bertelsen, the son of Gertrude Diederich, my grandfather's sister who had married Hans Claudius Bertelsen, a Danish immigrant farmer, in 1885 in Masterton. Their eldest son Claude was one of seven children and only 22 years of age when he died for his country at Gallipoli fighting the Turks.

"Of the five sons of Mr. H.B. Morpeth, town clerk of the small gold mining town of Waihi, who had attained military age, four enlisted for active service, and a fifth, who offered for the front, was rejected owing to an injury to one of his legs", the *New Zealand Herald* noted at the time. The newspaper added:

"Three took part in the memorable landing of the Australian and New Zealand forces at Gallipoli that fateful day, April 25, 1915.

"Lieut. Nichol 'Nick' Morpeth and Private Gerald Tad Morpeth were wounded together shortly after the landing. Little was known as to the whereabouts or condition of Private Moore Morpeth who was attached to a different platoon. [Moore was] posted as missing [but] private letters to relatives of men who were fighting at Gaps Tepe, Gallipoli, made it clear he had been killed in action . . . That Moore aged 21 had given his life for King and country was later confirmed by the military authorities."

My Dad's sister, Auntie Winnie, later married Tad Morpeth. The brothers' letters home from hospitals and later again from Gallipoli illustrate what King and country meant at the time. The letters are uncomplaining, unselfish in their young authors' sacrifices on that strip of rugged Turkish coast at the approach to the Dardenelles.

The handwritten missives show a stoic acceptance of the duty to fight and if necessary die for King and country. They didn't question Winston Churchill's historic tactical error in planning the disastrous Gallipoli landing in the first place. They were also uncomplaining of the most atrocious conditions on those blood-soaked hills which became the closest thing to hell. There was even a gentlemanly respect for their enemy. Uncle Tad mentioned that he and his fellow troops regarded the Turks as "clean fighters."

The Morpeth boys were thus an example of the type of "Kiwi" (New Zealander) patriotism that prevailed during both World Wars I and II. Another volunteer who joined up with them in the 6th Hauraki Company, Auckland Infantry Battalion, was a well-born "Pommy" (English) remittance man, Private J. Nathaniel (Nat) Williams. His father, Sir Robert Williams, had sent Nat out to New Zealand to cool off his high living in England.

"Well, we asked for the steel, and we have got it now. It was a great day. I was hit in the elbow while I had my glasses to my eyes," 2nd Lieutenant Robert Nichol (Nick) Morpeth wrote home to his father from the Heliopolis Hospital in Cairo, describing his personal experiences during the landing. Extracts from his letter were published in Auckland's *New Zealand Herald*:

"We [the Sixth Haurakis] did not commence to disembark, till 11 a.m., so had a great view of the navy in action. They bombarded all the Turkish batteries that were protecting the entrenched positions. The troops were transferred to lighters, which were rowed silently towards the shore. One lone shot suddenly rang out, and then a perfect hail of machine gun and rifle fire followed. The enemy seemed to direct most of their fire on the boats. Meanwhile the troops were landing as fast and as best they could. They say that there were wire entanglements in the water, but I did not experience any. The beach was about 20 yards wide, then there was a steep bluff to scale, to climb one had to use his hands as well as his feet. The bluff was about 400 feet high, covered with scrub. On the top of the cliff was the Turks' first position. The Australians, with fixed bayonets, climbed hard, and on their approaching the summit of the cliff, the Turks retreated and took up their position about a mile and a half back. This gave their guns an opportunity . . . the shrapnel fire was experienced by many of us for the first time. We worked up a long diagonal ridge, and found a very thin line of Australians. The enemy positions were generally apparent but the actual men and machine guns could not be seen. The cover was good and their trenches were skillfully concealed."

The *Auckland Star* picked up the story, printing excerpts from a letter written by Tad Morpeth while recovering from his wounds in a hospital in Birmingham, England: "We worked up to the firing line, and Nick was looking through his field glasses—searching for the Turks—and crouching. He had exposed himself a bit, and I had got on to him about it. Nick muttered something, then he got one. I thought he was gone. He said he had been hit through the left arm. He told us where the sniper was that had fired, and an Australian said that he had got the sniper. It was a fair-size wound, and the arm was broken. I bandaged him up as well as I could with field dressing, and we went back into a Turkish trench about 70 yards to our rear. Just when we were dressing Nick in the firing line, Nat Williams raised himself up, and asked: 'How is he?' Nat got a bullet in his right breast, and rolled right over on his face. Later I asked Nat how he felt and he said 'Not too good,' and he asked if I could see where the bullet had come out. There was blood on his right side and back, almost level with his heart, but I could not see where the bullet came out, though I told him I could. I told Nat to crouch all he could. We got up and had gone about a yard, when he stumbled to the right, and fell forward out of my arms, murmured 'Oh!' and fell stumbling on his face. Then he rolled on his back. I took a step towards his head and got hit. It was just to the left of the pit of the stomach. I pressed both hands on it hard and sat down by Nat's head and spoke to him several times but he never moved or spoke again. Thirsty! Well, no one has any idea of thirst till he has been wounded." They had only been ashore in Gallipoli a couple of hours.

Nick recalled in his letter that, "All the wounded in my vicinity had to get down to the beach, but could not go down the ridge, because it was under heavy fire, consequently the wounded had to stick to a winding gully full of undergrowth, with sudden drops of six feet, and for most of the way with mud up to the knees. The wounded struggled and were helped down. This and waiting on the beach were the wounded's worst time I think. "On his way to the beach Nick met Col. McBean Stewart, [their commander] who was shot and killed a few minutes afterwards.

Uncle Tad returned Sept. 6, 1915 again to fight in Gallipoli. Within four month he had contracted enteric fever and was shipped aboard the hospital ship *Aquitania* to the same hospital in England where he had convalesced before. In June 1916 Tad returned to the battlefront, this time at the Somme in France where he was wounded in the leg three months later. Incredibly, he returned yet a fourth time to the front lines in France and this time he returned unharmed with the casing of one of the last shells to be fired in the war. It had been engraved with the words: "The Great War ended on the 11th hour of the 11th month 1918."

For the foregoing and other reasons, Anzac Day was thus always a very special commemoration for Australians and New Zealanders. It marked, some said, the day both countries came of age, became nations. However the excitement for me faded as I outgrew childhood and survived my war, World War II. Years later nevertheless, when I was *TIME Magazine's* bureau chief in Mexico City, the Australian ambassadors who served there would ask me to read the April 25th Anzac Day prayer at a little Anglican church in Mexico City. I did, and would recall those unforgettable faces of men during those dawn parades, men who had survived the horrors of Gallipoli and worse.

*   *   *

As children we were nurtured on the greatness of the empire and all that. Our own New Zealand was so new that it possessed none of the majestic past of Mother England, which dominated our learning and appreciation of history and literature.

Yet, at Makara, we managed to find old shepherds' huts and campers' sheds that harbored curious links to and souvenirs from the past. In a corner of the Hawkins hayloft, over the milk shed, I discovered still clearly readable copies of the *Auckland Weekly News* magazine, dated from 1914 to 1918, with extensive pictorial coverage of the Great War. For some reason, perhaps out of respect, the rats had left the magazines alone. There were pages and pages of battle scenes and progress reports on the war which taken together, concluded that New Zealanders had been the deciding factor in defeating the Kaiser and the Turks. I invited others to my reading room in the corner of the hayloft, to enjoy an early, nationalistic-oriented history lesson.

CHAPTER 17

From Germany with Love

The photograph of Grandpa Bernard Joseph Diederich as a young man, rakish and debonair seated before a landscape painting, was taken in 1884 in the Wellington studios of Bill Baker, a local painter of some note. The painting was a beautiful oil rendering of the Mitre Peak dominating the Milford Sounds. Grandpa had biked all the way down the South Island and back. He was himself an accomplished artist and had painted the picture with which he was photographed; that year one of his works was exhibited in New Zealand's National Art Gallery. In the 1884 photograph, resplendent in waistcoat and tie and holding his paintbrush and palette at the ready, the young Diederich wore a mustache and had a lively twinkle in his eyes.

The Grandpa Diederich I got to know during his latter years was a kind-hearted man, methodical and the complete opposite of my Irish grandfather. There was nothing stereotypically Germanic about him. Nor did he drink, smoke or swear. He doted on his wife and even shared in the housework after she fell sick in 1929 and remained bedridden for the rest of her life with, it was suspected, tuberculosis and then rheumatoid arthritis. Nana Diederich had been sick for as long as I had known her. She lived in a special room at the front of the house which was filled with sun most of the day. He was a devout Catholic who attended church regularly and had no discernible interest in outright luxuries, although as a furniture-maker he lived well.

In the old Gray and then the Essex automobile in which we made the first trips there, it was as if the town of Palmerston North

were the other side of the moon, rather than a hundred miles from
Wellington. But the trip was always worth it. Grandpa was also
very different from our rough-edged neighbor farmers. He had
none of the gruffness of our Irish relatives who, when asked any
innocent question such as, "What's that?," would often snap sar-
castically: "It's a wigwam for a goose's bridle!" Or who would break
into song or recite a story of dear old Ireland, making jest of even
death. Grandpa Diederich's answers were patient, gentle and understanding.

And the countryside surrounding Palmerston North was so
different from the ruggedness of Makara. There were sheep and
cattle of course but they grazed on beautiful flat, lush, green
pastureland. This was one of the lovelier parts of New Zealand.
Some fields however were still scarred with the huge, ugly trunks
of native trees having been burned black, stark symbols of the
slash-and-burn method of clearing the country's primeval forests.

It was a great event for us youngsters to spend the weekend at
Grandpa Diederich's big house at 116 Linton Street, which in spring
was surrounded with its cherry blossoms. The streets of Palmerston
North were neat and flanked by homes framed by kaleidoscopic bushes
of flowers. Passion fruit hung from a tree outside the window of our
guestroom. It was a pretty town. Marking the center of each of the
town's main intersection, quaintly enough, was a huge imitation of a
fried egg—with the white at least five feet in diameter, and the yellow
yoke about six inches high. It was never explained whose idea it was
but the eggish intersection has since disappeared.

Grandfather Diederich still had a slight German accent that
was muffled as it sifted through his luxuriant mustache. He would
take me, as a child, sitting on the bar of his bicycle to milk his cow,
which he kept in a paddock not far from the Linton Street family
home. He taught us German nursery rhymes. And every Sunday,
after Mass, he would make a grand breakfast of large sausages smoth-
ered in rich gravy. An energetic and ingenious man, he once bi-
cycled down the South Island, in the process got 20 tire punc-
tures, and when the handlebar of his bike broke, he replaced it
with a willow stick.

Grandpa Diederich had come out to New Zealand as a boy of seven in 1876 from Germany, where he was born in Caternberg in 1868. (Caternberg is close to Stoppenberg which then was two miles north of the city of Essen. In a 1908 German directory of towns and places, Stoppenberg was described as a village in the Prussian administration of Dusseldorf belonging to the province of Essen.) Grandpa was baptized a Catholic, five days after his birth, in the neighboring village church in Stoppenberg.

Family trees suffer from uprooting and ancient documents don't always correspond to the facts. During World War II, for example, when the U.S. Coast Guard issued my security clearance pass, it described my person as having blue eyes and blonde hair, even though the photo on the pass clearly showed that I had dark hair and dark brown eyes. No guard at the San Francisco or Oakland docks and the Brooklyn, New York, Navy yards ever noticed.

Grandpa was the fifth child of Caspar and Gertude Diederich. Caspar had been born in 1828, the year after his parents Caspar Diederich and Mary Labour had married. Our great-grandmother Gertude Kohnen was born in Eschweiler, a German town close to the Belgian border and also near the town of Aachen, which was made famous during the early Middle Ages because Charlemagne was crowned there. It was in Eschweiler that Caspar Diederich II, our great-grandfather (his name was also noted as Kaspar on official German documents), and Gertrude had married on July 19, 1856. Caspar Keller was best man and Gertrude Hillebrand was matron of honor. Our great-grandmother Gertrude was the daughter of Carl Kohnen and Gertrude Primpler.

Although many of my family's German roots remain lost in time, there is one legend according to which an ancestor—a general in the Prussian army—had come to grief in a dispute with Prince Otto Von Bismarck after or before the Franco-Prussian war. Bismarck was at the height of his power as Reich Chancellor and Prussian Prime Minister.

In 1873 the German Empire had banned the Jesuit order together with the entire Roman Catholic church, and the Catholic clergy had been placed under the supervision of the state. Caspar

may have, as a good Catholic, considered himself an enemy of the
Reich and decided it was time to find a new, more tolerant home.
In fact it is still a bit of a mystery why they all came to New
Zealand at the particular time they did. The story of Bismarck not
being a family friend did arise during my childhood.

The early Diederichs seemed to have lived for a long period in
a suburb of Essen. In the yellowing family photographs my great-
grandfather Diederich, with his long flowing beard, looked a bit
like a rabbi, but Grandpa proved to be a staunch practicing Roman Catholic who took his religion very seriously and fasted during Lent. He did a great amount of charity work too and helped
the church by carving several beautiful wooden pulpits. He was
never known to miss Mass.

It was Grandpa's belief that Germany should play no part in our
lives—that was even before World War II broke out, when he firmly
damned Hitler to hell. He refused to speak German and only when
we were very young did he sing to us those German nursery rhymes.
He insisted that English was our language. Grandpa's reluctance to
speak of Germany meant we learned very little from him about Germany and the Diederich family's pre-New Zealand history. The little
he told us of his boyhood in Germany consisted of amusing events
such as the day in a restaurant with his father when he pulled out a
sausage that had been stuck in a roasted suckling pig the waiter was
carrying proudly into the room. The removal of the sausage released a
fountain of gravy onto the patrons.

The police certificate from Waltenscheit, written in old Gothic
German script, and which enabled them to leave Germany, notes
that Caspar Diederich was 5 feet 3 inches tall, age 46 in 1875,
and had blonde hair and gray eyes and no special marks. The police document states that it was signed by Kaspar Diederich from
Deckendorf who "has the intention of emigrating with his family,
Frau, formerly Kohnen, and his eight children to New Zealand in
England." In brackets "Australia" was inserted. The German authorities were obviously mystified as to the actual location of New
Zealand—not many Germans were migrating to the South Pacific
at that time.

The document goes on to state that Kaspar had asked for the necessary passport and that there was no objection to issuing the necessary travel papers, good for one year. The police document was dated November 18, 1875. Caspar (or Kaspar) Diederich and the family were then living in Gelsenkirchen where the last of their five daughters, Bertha Catharine, had been born in 1872.

Another son, Wilhelm, Grandpa's younger brother, died in Gelsenkirchen before the rest of the family could set off to catch the ship in Hamburg. (In 1954 I went to Gelsenkirchen only to find that its archives had been destroyed by a World War II Allied bombing raid. The town located close to Holland, did sport a "Diederich Brewery" and, given my father's enjoyment for good beer, the brewer just might have been a relative. (At a garage on the outskirts of the town I found a friendly German navy veteran of the North African campaign who, when he heard that I hailed from New Zealand, refused to accept payment for repairs to my car. He had captured—at least his fast ship had—a group of New Zealand soldiers swimming in the nude off the coast of North Africa. "We cut them off from the shore and they became instant POW's," he said. "Fine fellows and good swimmers.")

Mourning the death of young Wilhelm, the Diederich family of nine traveled to Hamburg and boarded the 1000-ton *Terpsichore*, a sturdy, full-rigged sailing vessel. They were going to the new land as part of the scheme of Sir Julius Vogel to introduce some hardy Northern Europeans to New Zealand's mostly English, Scottish and Irish population. (A footnote to this family history is the fact that our German ancestors might never have left Germany and gone to New Zealand if it had not been for the farsighted immigration policy of Vogel who had himself been born into a london middle-class Jewish family and migrated to New Zealand as a young man. Vogel began as a reporter and later moved up to become a newspaper publisher in the South Island. He became the British Colony's colonial secretary in 1868 and was later Premier of New Zealand. As Premier, he raised loans to pay for the transportation and settlement of immigrants in New Zealand. Vogel saw immigration as the only means of building a new nation and as New Zealand was competing with Australia and the United States for immigrants he decided to make an offer to Northern Europeans). It was a very small number, but it was a very small country.

The ship on which the Diederich's sailed became a virtual Tower of Babel with the 397 immigrants aboard speaking eight different languages, but mainly Danish, Polish, and German. In fact Caspar Diederich and his family were joining the first important wave of true immigrants who set out with their children to make a new life in the strange, far-off land where wars with the native Maori tribes were finally coming to a close. The earlier wave of settlers had been mostly whalers, sealers, soldiers, or gold-seekers. Many of these adventurers had moved on to seek gold or greener pastures elsewhere.

Our paternal great-grandparents brought with them their entire remaining brood: Johann, born in 1858; Catharina (Kate,) born in 1859; Marie, born in 1862; Gertrude, born in 1866 in France; Bernard Joseph, born in 1868; Elizabeth Frances, born in 1871; and Bertha Catherine, born in 1872.

The ship was towed down the Elbe on the evening tide on a cold November evening in 1875. There is no mention of the Diederich family's being involved in any of the shipboard shenanigans during the four-month trip down the Atlantic, around the Cape of Good Hope, across the Indian Ocean, and finally into the Tasman Sea and New Zealand.

The ship's Prussian doctor, Max Buckner, left his impressions in a journal that found its way to the Turnball Library in Wellington, and which was translated from the German into English. The doctor-surgeon explained that his duties encompassed not only caring for the sick but, "I also had the responsibility of ruling what amounted to a miniature republic." He was assisted in his office by a schoolmaster for the children, a matron to supervise single girls, and four constables who had to supervise the tidiness and cleanliness of the single men and families.

The peace in the floating polyglot miniature republic was endangered by the fact that the Danes hated the Germans. Dr.

Buckner stressed several times in his journal, "Germany, Bohemia, and Poland remonstrated but stubborn little Denmark conquered, while Germany wept and Bohemia and Poland shrieked." It was suggested after several ships arrived in New Zealand that the Germans and the Danes did not make good traveling companions, and where possible it was recommended that they not travel together to avoid friction. In fact, some Danes were refugees from an area seized by the German empire.

Yet in New Zealand the German-Danish friction appears to have dissipated, as Gertrude Diederich, who was ten years old when she arrived in Wellington, later married farmer Hans Claudius (Jack) Bertelsen at Saint Patrick's Catholic Church in Masterton in 1885.

Bertelsen was thirteen years her senior, and hailed from Denmark. Interestingly Great-Aunt Gertrude had been born in Alsace-Lorraines before it became, in 1871, part of the German empire. Her birthplace was in fact France.

The doctor also notes that the Scandinavians and Poles were "deadly enemies." There were likewise Catholics and Protestants, and competition between them when one group started their hymns. There was a school aboard ship, but even though there was an "excellent textbook designed for immigrants from an English speaking nation . . ." it hardly served this mixture of languages and nationalities on a German ship. The doctor assisted the birth of five babies during the trip. And in mid-January he faced the cursed disease of the time, typhus. After two months at sea the humidity and heat of the tropics brought the virus to life, and the first victims were "two strong young women, a Pole and a Dane." They prayed for cold weather. On the 132-day trip, a total of five adults and two children died of the epidemic.

On March the 20, 1876 they finally sighted the coast of New Zealand. They were the first of the family to glimpse Makara Beach as the ship rounded the headland into Wellington. When they finally arrived in Port Nicholson Harbor and sited the capital city, their journey had not ended. They were relegated to be quarantined on Somes Island in the middle of the harbor.

The long voyage ended literally with a bang when the *Terpsichore's* bosun decided to salute their arrival by firing off an "old rusty mortar." The *New Zealand Times* reported the contretemps stating, "A painful accident occurred on board the ship TERPISCHORE which arrived in port on Saturday morning. As the ship entered the harbor the customary preparations were made for firing the salute. One shot was fired, and the gun was charged again for the second, but before charging it the boatswain, who was superintending the operation, had neglected to sponge the gun, the consequence being that as he was ramming home the charge it exploded. The boatswain's hand was severely burnt, his little finger completely blown off, and the fleshy part of his arm was torn for about five inches. One of the passengers who was stopping the vent was severely burnt in the face. Both men were placed under the doctor's hands, and received prompt attention."

So the Diederich family finally made it to dry land. Yet, along with the demoralized other immigrants, had to wait out the passing of the typhus epidemic even as two immigrants died and were buried on Somes Island.

Finally, after two weeks on the little island, the Diederich family was allowed ashore. They were issued muskets along with powder and musket balls with which to protect themselves in case of another Maori uprising. To reach their land grant of some 40 acres at a place called Rangatumai in the Wairarapa Valley, they had to take a horse-drawn coach and learn that New Zealand, whatever its other primitive characteristics, was not backward in collecting bridge tolls. A toll gate over the Waiohine River cost one shilling and six pence for the horse and carriage plus six pence for each additional horse and one penny for a sheep or goat. To cross on foot cost two pennies.

Their land itself was covered in bush. The giant *rimu* and *totora* trees stood like natural fortresses that the family had first to conquer before they could farm the soil. The fate of the great trees was sealed by fire. They were burned down and their blackened stumps removed by hand. John and Bernard Joseph, together with their father and sisters, went to work to clear the land and build a home.

Their mother by all accounts was a formidable woman who was described by my father as "unafraid of work or anything."

In sum, the Diederich family were genuine pioneers who suffered all the hardships of the daunting bush land so different from the European surroundings they had left behind.

John [Johann] who was seventeen and the eldest offspring in the family was the first to marry. In 1884 John wed Mary Katherine McNamara at St. Mary's of the Angels Catholic church in Wellington. The McNamara family had migrated to New Zealand from India where Mary had been born in Poonamalle, Madras. For a time John and his wife lived on Nelson Street, in Wellington, where their first child Florence Gertrude Neville, was born. New Zealand was entering a depression and John was lucky to find work as a laborer. But after five years John and his wife, like a lot of new settlers decided to move to Australia where they sought better opportunities. In Australia they had two more children, Winifried (1890) and Mabel(1894).

It appears that Mary persuaded her husband that they should move to Madras, India, where she had been born and where he found work as an assistant to an engineer. In 1900 Mary died in India and John continued to raise the children. Then in 1902 at age 44 he married his children's 20-year-old music teacher, Katherine O'Brien Arbuthnott, at a ceremony in St. Mary's cathedral, Madras. (Our family for years preserved a photograph taken in India of the beautiful young Anglo-Indian bride and the short and dapper John.) Two more children were to follow from John's second marriage, John Bernard (1903) and Norah in 1908. The following year the family sailed to Ceylon and then back to Fremantle, the main port of Perth, Australia, where John had lived previously. In Australia four more children were born to John and Katherine. In time our family in New Zealand lost contact with John and his family in Western Australia.

There were few schools in those days but Grandpa, Bernard Joseph Diederich, and brother John along with the girls managed to get an early education in Germany, further teaching aboard ship, and additional schooling at home. Grandpa recalls as a child learning his lessons seated on a wooden log before their house. By age 12 Grandpa was busy working full-time on the family farm, and at 14 he went to Wellington as an apprentice cabinet maker for five shillings a week. As his board and lodging were going to cost him six shillings a week, he made an arrangement with the proprietor of the boarding house by which, in lieu of paying board, he got up early, lit the fire, prepared breakfast for his fellow boarders and did other chores.

On weekends he often rode his bicycle home over the Rimatuka hills, braving the wind that often blew riders off the summit, and returned Sunday night with eggs and cheese from the farm. He pedaled over 50 miles.

Winning the trust of his regular employer, Grandpa Diederich was allowed to keep the apprentice's cabinet-making tools with him and he set about making small cabinets on his own which he sold. One day, much later, while a young man, he was working in the Bank of New Zealand putting up cords in the windows. The bank manager, a Mr. Knox, noted the exacting way that the young man worked. "I've been watching you," the bank manager said. "You work diligently. Why don't you go into business for yourself and renovate houses?" Grandpa Diederich was quick to respond.

With the backing of the banker, Grandpa bought two houses on Te Aro Street for 600 pounds apiece, repaired them and resold them for 1,200 pounds each. On Austin Street he found two houses and two stores in need of renovation, and purchased them, and then he built a new house on Murphy Street. Eventually he set up his furniture shop on Cuba Street.

One day in 1898 he saw a young lady while attending Mass at St. Mary's of the Angels Church in Wellington. He found out who she was—Miss Rebecca Scanlon, whose father had a wine and spirits shop and was also a tea merchant. Grandfather Diederich introduced himself and a courtship followed.

The German-born immigrant, then 30 years old, married the New Zealand-born Irish lass of 24, and they peddled off on a tandem bicycle on their honeymoon to Wanganui, along that lovely river in the center of the North Island. (It was the first time the local Maoris had seen two persons riding one behind the other on a bike and the juxtaposition caused quite a stir around Wanganui.) Given his business vocation as an artist-craftsman with wood, Bernard Joseph had little time for his non-vocational art, painting, once he married. Even so, he won first prize in a 1900 exhibition in Christchurch with an artistically designed dining room sideboard made of New Zealand hardwood. The prize money was an impressive 100 guineas. Money however was not a problem for the young couple and they went on to have nine children, seven of whom survived.

After he married, grandfather moved his new wife into his two-story house at 107 Cuba Street which he shared with his parents. It was a large compound with a shop in front which was both the showroom and sales room for his furniture, which was made in another building in the back yard. Great-Grandfather Caspar and wife Muta lived upstairs. Caspar, wearing an embroidered velvet smoking jacket and a cap with a tassel, and puffing a meerschaum pipe, would stride up and down Cuba Street, one of the capital's principal arteries, as if he owned it. He died in 1893 and his tomb has a large ornamental cross. My father, christened Bernard John, the first child of Grandfather Diederich and the former Rebecca Scanlon, was born on Cuba street in 1898.

Grandpa Diederich prospered as a master furniture craftsman to the point where he constructed a large home on Waterloo Street in Lower Hutt. It was a spacious place with a water fountain and its own pumping system, a true villa. However, he subsequently suffered a series of adversities. He lost the furniture shop in a fire and the insurance company refused to pay for the loss. Earlier he had remarked, jokingly, to a neighbor, "I should burn it down," when the neighbor commented on the disorderly look of the old-fashioned workshop. The neighbor testified that he had heard Grandpa say he should burn it down. It didn't matter that all the evidence pointed to an accidental fire; the neighbor's testimony was enough for the insurance company to deny the claim.

Grandpa Diederich was tiring of Wellington, New Zealand's bustling capital city, anyway and decided that he should give it all up and become a farmer; he envisioned a fine farm on which his large brood of children could grow up and enjoy the countryside. He invested virtually everything he had left after the disastrous fire, in a 300-acre farm spread over choice land at Raumai in the Manawatu Valley not far from Palmerston North. However it turned out that the property had a mortgage, he had nothing in writing, and he lost the whole farm. He had been manipulated by an unethical lawyer.

At 45 years of age with a large family, Grandpa Diederich, undaunted, began again in the furniture business, in Palmerston North. It was August 1913—one year to the month before the start of World War I.

I was privileged, years later, to watch Grandpa at work in his furniture shop. He was an authentic artisan who loved his craft. On his rare trips to Makara he would look at our rolling surf and turn away. I often wondered whether it was a painful reminder of that long and unpleasant sea voyage from Hamburg to New Zealand. It was obvious that it had given him a life long aversion to the sea.

One day in 1950, Grandpa Diederich had just finished fashioning a large pulpit for a new church. He helped carry the pulpit inside and set it up in the church. He went home and said he thought there was something wrong with him and asked for the standard cough cure: hot water. He died in his sleep of a blood clot in the heart. He was 83 years of age and he had never seen a doctor in his life.

There is a footnote to Grandpa Diederich's saga discovered by Beverley Burt, nee Bertelsen while researching her Diederich roots:

Grandfather after World War One learned he was an alien and he had to file an application to become a New Zealand. In his letters of application he explained the reason he had not applied for Naturalization before 1922 was that he had always believed his father had been naturalized and that the whole family had automatically become New Zealanders.

In a letter dated 22/10/22 Grandpa explained that he had not only served in the Masterton Volunteers for several years but also that he had as a good citizen been called upon to serve on juries during his adult life. He also noted that his eldest son served in the Police force in Christchurch). Nor did he mention that his wife was New Zealand born and that he had been a tax payer, never had a mark against his character, and never been charged with a crime in his life. The official government reply noted that as Bernard Joseph Diederich "is a native of Germany and in respect thereof could not be granted materialization unless he or their immediate relatives have served abroad with the British forces."

Grandpa replied that his eldest son (our father) was not of military age while the war was on however three of his nephews had served with the New Zealand forces. They were Claude Bertelsen (killed in action at Gallipoli) Bernard Edwin Bertelsen and Leo Welch. As a result of this letter, grandfather' memorial was referred to the Stipendiary Magistrate for recommendation. On Nov.10, 1922, after an exchange of additional letters, Grandpa signed the Oath of Allegiance to the crown, and was gazette six days later as a British subject and New Zealand citizen.

What would have happened if grandfather had not had three nephews serving in the Great War? Denied naturalization would he have had to return to Germany and leave his sons and daughters in New Zealand? It illustrated just how provincial the New Zealand government department of immigration had become in the wake of the Great War. After 56 years in New Zealand, a country that had invited him there in the first place as an immigrant, he was being denied citizenship because he was born in Germany. Had anyone cared to take this further any persons who had been convicted of a crime when he had sat on the jury, that person would have been entitled to declare a mistrial and be let out of prison on bail pending another trial.

CHAPTER 18

Our Rose of Tralee

There is grist for a harlequin romantic novel or a TV mini-series in the life of our Irish great grandparents on our father's side of the family.

There are a lot of questions that our family lore did not address in this enthralling mid-19th century love story.

How my siblings and I wished we had known our paternal great-grandmother, Maria Teresa Hurly Scanlon from Tralee in County Kerry, Ireland. No letters or journals have survived only the oral hand-me-downs of that remarkable woman's odyssey. Maria was our heroine. She married the man she loved against her parents, spent the next decade apart from him and eventually went in search of him. Her love quest took her literally to the end of the earth, the Antipodes.

Our great-grandfather Patrick Charles Scanlon also hailed from County Kerry and his family farmed at Kilmore, near the Hurly country home. Patrick was born there in 1832. A tall, strong and handsome schoolteacher, Patrick was the son of Edmund Scanlon and the former Honora Eliza Whelan. Patrick had completed his studies in Dublin. The Scanlons were a very devout old Roman Catholic family with deep ancestral roots.

The Hurly who could trace their ancestry to the Munster Kings were not all Protestants.

Ireland was under London's harsh rule, and Catholicism was outlawed. Our family counted as an ancestor the Catholic archbishop of Cashel. Educated in France the archbishop had returned to Ireland to preach clandestinely and say masses secretly. Discovered by the British, he was given "The Boot," a special treatment reserved for practicing Catholics. Tin boots were filled with boiling oil and the archbishop's feet were fitted into them. Being Irish he survived the English boot.

No doubt Maria's family would have given the boot or worse if they had caught up with Patrick Scanlon. But our great-grandfather was quick on his feet. .

Unknown to the uppity, wealthy Protestant John Hurly and his wife (the former Rebecca Burns), their daughter Maria had fallen head over heels in love with Patrick.

Dominated by the English, Ireland had not only a rigid caste system but also a good Irish Catholic would not think of marrying into a Protestant family. It seemed there was no way that Patrick, in spite of his excellent education in Dublin, could wed into the aristocratic Hurly family.

John Hurly was the local squire, Clerk of the Peace and J.P. for County Kerry. The Hurlys we were told had "conformed," i.e., become Protestant to keep their lands. It was assumed that when Oliver Cromwell's army rode roughshod over Ireland the Hurly family had moved to the side of the English. In the eyes of the Catholic Irish, we were told that it was the most unspeakable of crimes, to "conform."

Undeterred by his class status or religion, athletic Patrick would jump the fence while walking to church when he was secretly courting Maria. When he heard the news from Maria that a Protestant bridegroom had been sent for in Scotland, he rushed home to Tralee, jumped the fence of Kilduff House, the Hurly country home, and eloped with Maria. They were married in May 1860 at BallyMcElligot in Kerry. She was 20 and he was 28. If John Hurly had not been in his grave the wedding would have put him there.

Shortly after their marriage Patrick received word that his name was on the British wanted list of people suspected of belonging to the Fenians, or the Irish Republican Brotherhood, forerunners of today's Sinn Fein. Quickly and quietly he was smuggled out of Ireland along with a group of his countrymen headed for the gold fields of California.

We often wondered if Maria could have chosen to accompany him. She could not. The family explanation was that the gold fields of California were certainly no place for a pregnant lady. It was a mad place of men delirious with gold fever, a Pandemonium of armed and dangerous, often drunken, men and feisty prostitutes.

After the birth of her son Jeremiah (Jerry) Charles Scanlon in May 1861, Maria was offered a position as companion to a wealthy lady, Mrs Elvina Biss. Leaving her son Jerry with the Scanlon family in Tralee, Maria went to the United States in the employ of Mrs. Biss. Maria is said to have traveled to California but Patrick had already moved on to the gold fields of Australia. Whether the Biss family and Maria traveled across America to California by covered wagon or by sea is lost to history.

The gold trail led Patrick from Bendigo and Ballarat in Australia and finally to the new gold field of Gabriel's Gully in the South Island of New Zealand.

In 1863 the South Island of New Zealand was still a rugged, forbidding, and unpopulated land of high mountains, glaciers and dense forests. Added to the coast's negatives was the fact it was rough and dangerous with no natural harbors. Patrick was a strong man and he was quick to join the hundreds—later thousands—of gold-seekers who landed from Australia, United States and even China. He didn't fit the successful digger stereotype with money spent on looking good, hanging gold around his neck or fingers, and looking like the digger dandies of the day dressed in Crimean shirts, white moleskin trousers held up with a crimson silk sash, and knee-high boots and black sombreros. But as most good Irishmen he had a fondness in later life for the horses—race horses.

Like so many others who fought the elements in this inhospitable land in search of El Dorado, Patrick's journey had been more akin to the privations of the gold-seekers in the Alaskan gold rush. Along with two other men, he is credited with being the first European to traverse on foot—the only manner they could penetrate the bush and cross its many rivers—the main spine of New Zealand's South Island. There were hardly any Maoris in the area so there were no tracks to follow through the primeval forests. The trip, a major undertaking, was in search of gold, not to set records or survey the land or its wild life. They had to carry their supplies, as there was little to eat except native pigeons and heart of the Nikau palm and fern roots. It was a time when men afflicted with gold fever were prepared to make the ultimate sacrifice in their search.

Prospectors were striking out in twos and threes in their search. Some were swallowed up by the forest and fast flowing rivers and never heard of again.

Two prospectors, who managed to struggle up the uninhabited West Coast from the new town of Hokitika had camped one night in August 1866 by a little Creek which was later to be known as Candlelight creek. As one of the prospector held his "digger's lantern", a crude invention with a candle wedged into the neck of a transparent bottle from which the bottom has been removed, allowing his mate to safely reach down and fill the billy with water for their evening cup of tea, he let out a cry that was heard around the world. The lantern revealed that the bed of the creek literally shone with fine flowery gold. Neither man was afflicted with bush fever; they recognized real gold when they saw it. In the morning they began scooping gold out of what became known as Candlelight Creek.

The strike was on. Thousands of diggers working less profitable gold fields on the East Coast set out as soon as the news spread of a new and handsome strike in a place known to the Maori as Tauhinau described as a pakihi (grass) wasteland. Some drowned crossing mountain rivers while others collapsed and died of sheer exhaustion and hunger climbing through the bush-clad mountains to reach the Pakihi gold strike as they called it. Even more gold-seekers came from Australia, sailing across the South Tasman Sea.

Patrick Scanlon was one of those who made it to the new strike. Within a year a town sprang up on a sloping pakihi, grass country. The new town of calico and tents soon had its name changed from Pakihi to Charlie's Town and eventually Charleston. Some said the new town was named after a Scottish village on the Firth of Forth.

Others suggested it derived from Charlie Bonner the first name of the master of the 13-ton Ketch Constant, the first vessel to enter the dangerous little spoon-shaped inlet before the town. The inlet was named Constant Bay after Charlie's ketch. The big neighboring river was named The Nile, no relation to the great Egyptian river. That the town mushroomed so fast was even more remarkable because everything had to be brought in by ship. The town was landlocked. And hauling supplies through treacherous seas to Constant Bay was a test of wills and seamanship. The inlet was shallow and shaped like a bottle with its narrow neck leading to the sea, less than sixty feet across between jagged rocks.

Traveling by sea from Wellington, Nelson or Christchurch to Constant Bay was considered a dangerous high-risk voyage because the boisterous South Tasman Sea more than often makes it impossible to approach the rocky coast. More than a dozen ships had come to grief off Charleston and, even in Constant Bay, at least two dozen drowned in their effort to land on the beach. "The lure of gold made mariners forget about the reputation this Southwest coastline had," the brief history of Charleston relates. "Where previously they viewed it with mistrust and gave it a wide berth, they now ventured into the narrow entrance to the bay".

At the beginning, in 1866, so close to starvation were the miners they slaughtered the first bullock to be landed on the beach from the ship carry relief supplies. Within the time it took to start a fire the huge animal was being roasted in a spectacular beach barbecue. The welcome aroma of roast beef was said to have filled every tent and shack in the new town.

Gold eventually opened up this once lonely section of the West Coast and it became known as Westland. Diggers and packers finally found passes over the Southern Alps or scrambled ashore in the inlet when there was a brief respite from ferocious gales that swept the coast.

In order to aid maritime traffic the town setup a flagstaff on the bluff overlooking the bay's entrance. A signalman was provided with a cottage and rules to warn approaching vessels of the prevailing conditions in the bay. Strangely flag colors were reversed.

A red flag at the masthead signaled that conditions were favorable for a ship to enter the inlet. A blue flag warned the tide was out and a white flag signaled that it was far too dangerous to enter. It was without doubt the most dangerous and primitive port in New Zealand. Moorings inside the bay were a simple ringbolt set in a large rock on the beach. At low tide, providing there was no surf, the cargo was unloaded. There were also surfboats that aided, for a price, ships entering port with unloading of passengers and cargo.

In spite of its isolation, Charleston mushroomed into a real town overnight. The gold strike proved to be among the richest on the coast. While Candlelight creek quickly gave up its gold, strikes were found everywhere, even in the town, behind it and up the Nile River.

*   *   *

Maria meanwhile returned from America to Ireland to retrieve her son Jerry staying with the Scanlon family in Tralee. She was shocked when she saw him. A horse had kicked the little boy in the face. His nose was broken. It was never set. Jerry, a big lad at age nine, recalled their departure from Ireland. "All the family in Tralee was sitting around the kitchen table crying".

In 1870 Maria finally sailed for New Zealand, on the good ship *Lady Brown* to continue her search for her husband.

It may be difficult to believe the dramatic family story of Maria's search through the gold fields of the world after so many years without making contact. Both were highly literate persons and, while the mail was unpredictable, it was in existence. In 1866, coast-to-coast telegraphic communication between Westland and the much larger East Coast town of Christchurch had been established. But how can one contradict such widely repeated family lore without evidence to the contrary?

Charleston was an obvious choice to search for Patrick as the gold town was filled with fellow Irishmen most of whom had moved there from Australia.

In fact the Irishmen brought their religious division and dissension with them. Irwin Faris records in this book: *Charleston: Its rise and decline*: Among Westercoasters the story of the riot at Addison's is an oft-told tale, handed down from father to son. The *Westport Times* and *Charleston Argus* of April 4, 1868, records that the trouble occurred on the 2nd of the month.

"The *Hibernian Budget* of a comparatively recent date, states that the 'combined Hibernians' of the district had decided to hold a ball. As the Hibernian Society was not established in the district until January 1870, the reference probably should be to the 'Celtic Committee,' or to the Fenian Society. The *Hibernian Budget* continues: 'In those days dancing rarely ceased until daylight, and this occasion was no exception. After the ball the men gathered together in little groups in the street, and not very much further away were groups of Orangemen. The latter men offered a wager that a girl, Bella Newton by name, would not be permitted to ride a horse unmolested through the Hibernians. The girl accepted the wager, and having tied an orange handkerchief around her neck, she mounted a white horse and set off. As she passed through the ranks of the Hibernians they took her horse by the head and asked her the meaning of the exploit. Upon being informed that the ride was the result of a wager, they took the handkerchief from her neck and, facing the Orangemen, tore it to shreds. This was the signal for the commencement of a first-class riot. News of the battle quickly spread from north to south, and men both orange and green flocked to take sides at Addison's. It is reported that there was not a pick-handle nor an axe-handle to be purchased within a wide radius of the town."

Patrick Scanlon was said to have taken great pleasure in fighting the Orangemen. He and his fellow Greens forced the Orange to retreat into a swamp and the riot turned into a mud fight. A true Irish donnybrook. The hostilities were finally brought to an end with the arrival and intervention of the Chief Warden of the province.

It was two years after the riot that Maria crossed from Wellington to the East Coast of the South Island. From the very English town of Christchurch, mother and son took the long and hazardous bouncing stagecoach ride over the Southern Alps to Westport. It was the last leg of her epic journey in search of her beloved husband, and it was the most precarious. In spite of the majestic beauty of the snow-capped Alps, the view from the crowded stagecoach was mostly of bottomless ravines. Any mishap could have sent them crashing to their deaths. Even worse in the family's eyes, was the fact that Maria was still a protestant. She could not hope to go to heaven. The jarring, jolting journey could also impair the passenger's health leaving them with permanent body injuries. Yet Maria and Jerry were already sturdy pioneers and expected the trip to be rough.

Maria's objective was Charleston. By 1870 it had become a well-established town but difficult to reach. Only 25 kilometers away from Westport, where Maria and Jerry arrived on the West Coast, the gold town was still hours away. A small booklet entitled *Charleston The Way it Was* explains: "The Old Beach Route, joining Westport with Charleston, was used from 1867 until it was abandoned in 1874. The old route was by today's standards an arduous journey-taking about three hours on horseback or about eight hours for wagons to cover the 22 miles."

The brief history of Charleston continues: "People started from the South Spit with goods and luggage after they had been ferried across the Buller River battling the tidal and often moody river. The ferryboats, of which there were about thirty, left Westport from Bull's steps and landed at some steps near Waterman's Arms Hotel. People, horses and wagons traveled seven miles of beach (Carters Beach) to Cape Foulwind—about seven miles over the Cape where the road cuts through bush—over another short beach at Tauranga Bay—through a short cutting of shrub only the northern end of the Nine Mile Beach—traveled along this beach to the mouth of the Totara River to be ferried across and continue down the beach, terminating with a piece of road through bush—over a bridge on the Nile River—through a cutting—over a small hill and onto the town of Charleston. Along the way there were many places to break the journey. The first coach stop at the end of Seven Mile Beach was Gibson's, a small store and wayside house.

On the northern edge of Tauranga Bay stood the Halfway House Hotel. At the Totara River mouth (Okasri River) stood the Ferry House. After paying a shilling to cross, the next stop was Welcome Inn at the northern end of Little Beach—one of the best remembered hostelries in the district."

The family liked to imagine the extremely emotional scene of the two lovers finally facing each other in Charleston. Oral family history is the storyteller and often chooses what to include and leave out. Fortunately this historic family scene had a witness: ten-year-old Jerry. It was, in his memory, anything but romantic. Patrick looked every bit a successful well-known dignitary of the town, dressed accordingly, with a frock coat and top hat.

Doffing his hat, Patrick greeted the beautiful 31 year-old Maria in the most staid Victorian manner. It was as if nothing had happened, as if their separation had lasted days, not an entire decade! "Welcome my dear Maria, your room is ready and waiting upstairs." Maria is said to have replied with a twinkle in her Irish eyes; "Thank you, dear Patrick." The father with a quizzical look inspected the son he had never met and noted his disfigured nose. He placed a hand on the boy's head ruffling his hair and laughed a happy laugh. Jerry grew up as "strong as an ox," wrestled and boxed and could shoe a horse and bend a horseshoe before he became an adult.

There was no other woman on the premises. No evidence that Patrick, 38-years-old tall and handsome, had been unfaithful to Maria. If he had "played around", his bachelor days, that day in 1870, were over for good. Maria was not about to let him out of her sight again.

An accomplished violinist, Patrick wooed Maria anew, serenading her with strings and rekindling the romance that evidently had never died, at least for Maria. The intriguing absence of ten years can only be explained by the fact that Patrick, by that time, had struck it rich, and could provide handsomely for a wife and family. The family began to grow immediately.

The Charleston that Maria and Jerry discovered, although only four years since its founding, had become a well-endowed town, nothing like the bad old frontier-gold mining towns. In fact it didn't live up to the boast as a town of 92 pub-hotels, where "Everyone who doesn't dig sells grog and everyone who digs hits the grog."

In his interesting 1941, *Charleston: Its rise and Decline,* author Irwin Faris recorded, "The population has been orderly and there has been little crime."

There was an Institute and library, St. Patrick's Catholic school and church, Methodist and Anglican churches, Freemasons' Lodge, an Oddfellows Lodge and branches of the Union, New Zealand, and New South Wales Banks, a fire station, post office and a resident surgeon, hospital and Catholic and Protestant cemeteries. Besides the dance halls—among them the "Royal Casino de Venice"—there were two newspapers, the *Charleston Herald* and the *Charleston Argus.* The editor of the *Charleston Herald,* Patrick Kitson, wrote many of his editorials in verse. The editor of the *Charleston Argus* was just as creative in his writings he was conscious of the mining community. Miners were not averse to making up their own verse and submitted it to the newspapers.

There was a pioneer bootmaker, Robert Hannah, who branched out to become New Zealand's main shoe store chain in later years. The population at one time reached 14,000. At least three breweries supplied the thirsty miners. There were several cops but few robbers.

The family story is that Patrick owned a general store and bakery on the East Side of North Camp Street. A family photograph shows Maria holding her current child standing before the store in about 1872. The store had the name Scanlon written in large letters over its portals. The first name appears to have been erased. Documents of the time confirm what a careful study of the photograph proves that the first name was Harold not Patrick. The identity of Harold Scanlan has remained a mystery. Documents also note that Patrick Scanlon was one of two "Grantees" of the store. Another explanation in the family was that Harold Scanlon left and Patrick took over the store, which later became the City Hotel.

One family rumor is that one of Patrick's brothers had joined him in New Zealand but fell out with him over a rich gold strike. They parted company and never spoke to each other again. The other brother even changed the spelling of their surname to Scanlan. (A New Zealand cousin, Brian FitzGerald, who made a personal search in Ireland notes that the spelling of Scanlon with an "a" or "o" is of little consequence, as some of the cousins in BallyMcElligott Parish are known by either spelling and they are certainly from the same stock/clan.)

For a while I suspected that Patrick's one time partner might have been his brother Michael Scanlon. There is no evidence that Michael came to New Zealand. However there is hardly any mention of Michael by the family. He had been born in 1830 and was two years older than Patrick. I often wondered why the family knew so little about him. His death is not noted on the family tree or that of his wife. And the strange fact that has come to light is that at the age of 18, he also married a Hurly! Caramba!

On December 18,1848, when John Hurly, my great-great grandfather was still alive and kicking, young Michael had married Hurly's daughter Frances (Fanny) Hurly in BallyMcelligott, County Kerry! Fanny was Maria's older sister. Their marriage must have provoked the first heated Hurly-Scanlon scandal. Surely, they too had eloped.

The family seemed to have completely overlooked this controversial wedding between a young Hurly lady and young Michael Scanlon. They had two children, according to cousin Maureen Riegman in Auckland, another family tree hunter. Michael and Fanny's daughter, Mary Ann came to New Zealand and married Jerrmiah Curtain. Their daughter, born in 1877 in Mount Fyfe, Kairoura in the South Island of New Zealand, entered Holy Orders in 1900 and became Sister Mary Brendan of the Order of Mary. Interestingly her cousin, Honora Maria Scanlon, Patrick and Maria's second daughter helped Sister Brendan in her duties as a nun. Honora had taken the name Sister Benignus. The two cousins devoted their lives to teaching at St Mary's Convent Girl's school in Wellington. As a youngster I recall meeting Auntie Sister Brendan at St. Mary's and how I wished I had known enough to asked her about her father and Fanny Hurly and when they came to New Zealand. Sister Brendan died in 1941.

Cousins in New Zealand were lucky to have managed to trace most of the ancestors considering that most of the records at Ballycelligott and Tralee were burned during the Black and Tan war as they were in Tralee. When Maria died, a letter of condolence arrived from Limerick, Ireland signed J. Hurly Scanlon.

There was another Scanlon also named Michael in Charleston. Michael Scanlon, and an associate, Maloney, had a butcher shop on the Road to Back Lead, the name for one of the operating gold digs. (Curiously enough, he left Charleston to go into business in Westport in 1875, about the same time that Patrick Scanlon decided to move his family to Wellington.

Michael Scanlon, the butcher, first took over the Black and White Hotel in Westport, and later established a much more profitable ironmonger store (Hardware business.) His hardware shop grew into one of the river port town's most successful businesses. But his descendants who knew little of their pioneer ancestors' origins, at least did know that he hailed from a town called Quinn in County Clare. He died in Westport at aged 54 and was definitely not a County Kerry Scanlon.

Among Patrick's occupations was that of purchasing gold for at least one of the several Banks established in the town. Under the early form of government of the Karamere, the family records that he had distinguished himself as the first superintendent of the town of Charleston. More importantly, at least to him, were his efforts to launch horseracing, a sport close to his and most of his fellow Irishmen's heart. He became clerk as well as steward of Charleston's horse races. The first important race was held nearby on nine-mile beach beginning in 1869. By 1871 horses were brought in from as far away as Auckland to compete in the local races, and the stakes were high for those days.

Everyone attended the horse races. They were the social the events of the season. As the oft-repeated saying went in New Zealand: "On the turf, and under it, all men are equal." Whether Charleston had the first race course is disputable but it certainly was one of the first.

The year after Maria's reunion with Patrick in Charleston, a second son was born:

Edward Patrick on August 18, 1871. Next to be born was my grandmother, Rebecca on October 6, 1873, and then Honora Maria on August 10, 1875.

It was that year that Patrick decided it was time to move to the capital. Gold was running out and the population and businesses had begun to decline. The miners knew that Charleston's raison d'être was gold, and without gold it would disappear. Patrick was sufficiently wealthy to move his family and launch a new business in the capital. The Nile bridge leading to Westport was washed away in a particularly bad storm in 1874. But when the Scanlon family, numbering six, bid good-byes to Charleston, they crossed the Nile River on the brand new suspension bridge, the first ever built in New Zealand.

Behind, they left the snow covered Paparoas and striking scenery of the Nile Valley. Ahead lay the crowded windy city, Wellington. No longer would the tormented Tasman Sea lull the children to sleep.

In the capital Patrick and Maria added three more children to their brood: Elvina Mary, Margaret Josephine and John Joseph.

*   *   *

A 137 years later we spent a delightful Southern Hemisphere Indian summer in Westland—known for its cruel winters. Even the seals were basking in the sunshine. Shimmering Constant Bay, where passengers schooners had been wrecked and some two dozen persons drowned trying to reach shore, was placid as a lake. We were motoring alongside the lazy blue Tasman under a warm March sun in the year 2001, giddy from the majesty of this demi-paradise of my native land. The Franz Joseph and Fox glaciers, as well as Mount Cook were awe-inspiring. Considering the first Pakeha (white man) on the South Island was a New England sealer, it was a delight to see scores of seals peacefully sunbathing on rocks while their cubs splashed in the rising surf. Dwelling on the beauty of it all, on that smooth highway to Westport from Hokitika, the greenstone capital of the world, we might have passed Charleston by if it had not been for fellow passenger, Ian Cross, who spied a sign illustrated with two diggers advertising a Charleston motel. A "No Vacancy" notice signaled our arrival.

The old Charleston was not even a ghost town. It had all but disappeared. Only the cemeteries outside town remained. A new hotel stood by the main road. Two motels were filled with film crews and actors working on making "The Lost World," a seemingly appropriate title for Charleston, itself a lost world much like the film of the dinosaurs in Conan Doyle's book. The fabulous scenery was also used as a backdrop for a now famous movie, "The Lord of The Rings."

This was a world I would have loved to know. I had asked many New Zealanders whether they could tell me about Charleston, once the richest town in the country. Few could. They said they had heard of it but didn't know where it was. The three-story European Hotel, the last of Charleston's many hotels that stood as proof of the past, had finally succumbed to time and the wrecker's ball forty years earlier. Surrendering to my emotions I trod the weeds where Patrick Scanlon's store once stood. It was curious that the surface of the ferocious Constant Bay was like a mirror with not the slightest suggestion of surf running. Only as we left, the rustle of a slight breeze reminded us that the civilization of yesteryear, built on gold, was not always as peaceful as during that beautiful sunny day.

Nature has reclaimed its own, covering the scars of man's greed for gold. The Nile Valley and river offer some of the most overwhelmingly beautiful scenery in the world. For that reason, a film crew was they're filming as a substitute for the Amazon basin Conon Doyle's "The Lost World."

There is still a glitter of hope for the town long dead. One person figuratively trying to keep the digger's lantern lit is artist Diane Malibu who lives in her post-gold era home at 19 Princess

Street. With her paintings and documented maps of old Charleston, she can guide visitors back in time.

Yet the Charleston area has not lost its magic. Today it boasts one of the finest eco-tour operations. There is also, yes underwater rafting, four hours of exciting adventure meandering through a calcitic Paradise of stalactites and stalagmites in caves in nearby Paparoa National Park. It includes a magnificent glow-worm-lit underground river.

*   *   *

Patrick became a wealthy Wellington wine, spirits and tea merchant, and retired at fifty. Later in life Patrick continued to wear his belltopper hat and frock coat, complemented by a white beard. He was a popular figure at the horse races. When he died the true story of his and Maria's romance died with him. Yet I always believed that Maria's story would have been the most interesting of all.

Maria quietly converted to Catholicism, which made her a Scanlon family saint. She died in 1896 at age 56 and is buried in Karori cemetery, where Patrick joined her in 1923 at the age of 91. My grandmother, Rebecca Scanlon, nursed her mother, and in her last year, she left the house only to attend Mass.

*   *   *

On our visit to Ireland in 1954, my mother and I found Jack Scanlon, who along with his two brothers, had sold their dairy farm in the Taranaki and returned to a free Ireland and married. Their home was a few miles east of Tralee. We arrived that late-spring day (June 11) to find relatives gathered to celebrate son Michael's first Mass the following day. Mother was thrilled and went to communion. When I looked back at the souvenir of Michael's ordination at Kilkenny on Pentecost Sunday, June 6, of the Marian year 1954, I noted that he spelled the family as Scanlan.

Jack took us to visit his mother's farm. She was a grand old lady, age 92, and insisted on singing Irish ballads before serving tea. (A member of the family handed me a baby bottle filled with milk, just like the bottle from which I fed their little foal on the Scanlon's farm in New Zealand. I then fed the Irish Piglet.)

Maria Hurly's former country home, Kilduff, was still standing, an imposing two-story structure. As an English couple occupied it, I stood in the garden and took photos of not only the house but also the battered remains of the Hurly coat-of-arms on the principal side of the house.

When John Hurly died, his son, Maria's brother, Robert Conway Hurly, J.P. inherited Bridge House in Tralee and the Glenduff (Kilduff) country home. Another son John took over Fenit House. Robert's son, John Conway Hurly, sold the property in 1912 and immigrated to Alberta, Canada. (The story related to my mother and me by relatives on the Scanlon side was that the Hurlys at Glenduff had indulged a little too much in their pleasures, horses and gambling. They were finally forced to sell this property. It was sold at auction but when John Conway Hurly heard that one of his enemies had bought it through the use of someone else's name, he lost control. Returning to his former home with a sledgehammer, he climbed a ladder and began smashing the family coat-of-arms to pieces. He was caught still up the ladder and arrested for defacing private property. Whether this was true or not it made a good story in the local pubs. In fact when Jack took us to the Four Elms, a little pub in the Irish bogs, we met more relatives, a Roche and a Glieson half-brothers who told us about Mrs. Fuller at Fenit whose late husband's mother was a Hurly. The Hurlys had had some splendid homes.)

In her diary, mother recounts:

"We left the hotel in Tralee after breakfast and drove to Fenit House. It was a delightful place and the occupant, a Mrs. Fuller whose husband's mother was a Hurly, greeted us and showed us photos. We thought John Hurly looked like Bernard. Later we realized that John was Bernard's Great-Great Grandfather. Mrs. Fuller told us to call on Colonel Hurly of the Indian army, as he had all the books as well as the family tree. Fenit fronts onto Tralee

Bay and had its own small dock. It was from this dock Mrs. Fuller's husband had gone fishing and never returned.

"After a picnic lunch in the Kerry countryside we drove on to Caragh Lake where the Colonel lives with his wife and son. Their son, Maurice, a doctor, was away in Dublin. They are charming people and have volumes about the Hurlys the first of whom was a king of Munster in 234 A.D. They seemed to have held titles, as there were photos of them in powdered wigs etc. The Colonel took Bernard into the study and showed him the family tree. Bernard was upset to learn that when Maria left home her branch of the tree was cut off! While Kilduff is out of the family now, Colonel Hurly said, Fenit house would revert to him if they cannot establish an heir when Mrs. Fuller dies. The Colonel and his wife promised to call on us when in London, so we took our leave.

"While in Tralee someone scraped off the little British flag on Bernard's new Morris Minor, that stated it was a 'British product'. I kept telling Bernard that his sweater was orange color and he insisted it was a shade of yellow. He learned I was right when he found it tightly rolled up into a ball of wool. Orange is not a favorite color in Ireland."

Today Glenduff is an attractive hotel and pub. The lands were sold off and the stableyards removed.

CHAPTER 19

Finally "The City"

J ust as I was getting used to Makara School I had to face up to
the wrenching transition of attending school in Wellington. It was
much like Dick Whittington and his cat going to London but my
self-confidence was on a par with that of the cat. I had finally
conquered the country. I didn't need the city.

My new school was The Marist Brothers' School at Thorndon
an old residential section of the Capital. The French Marist order
had been confirmed in 1836 by Pope Gregory XVI as the new
Society of Mary "to spread the Catholic faith, both by Christian
education of youth and by mission even in the remotest parts of
the earth." It was the French Marists who had founded the Roman
Catholic Church in New Zealand and they couldn't have found a
more remote country. Ironically the Catholic schools in New
Zealand, though founded by French clerics, taught predominantly
Irish students, as was the case at Marists Thorndon.

Marists Thorndon had a reputation as a rough and tough
school. Again Stellamaris and Quita, who were already attending
St. Mary's Convent in Wellington, one of the country's leading
Catholic girls' schools, put the fear of God into me about how
difficult—scholastically—I would find Marist. Brian was to follow me to Marist. It was a crowded boy's school. It was there that
I made my first Maori friends. From the old wooden building of
our Marist School, we could look out the classroom windows at
red-bricked St. Mary's girls' school across the street, a much more
refined and expensive institution.

Many of my classmates at Marist had never heard of Makara.

One fellow from Karori said it was "the tip," slang for a garbage disposal site, whereupon I angrily punched him. I suspected that his family was among those who had jettisoned their garbage at one time or another on Makara Hill. But our address nonetheless was so unusual as to be embarrassing—Brian and I were the only students from Makara. I would often give as our home address that of one of my aunts in Wellington.

Mum had the added burden of outfitting not only her girls in their black-and-white uniforms but also Brian and me in our traditional Marist colors, with knee socks, flannel shirt and jersey. We also had to wear a little cap that was known as a "cheese cutter." We wore short pants, which meant daily scrubbing of dirty knees.

Logistically, we had to coordinate our school commuting with Dad's machine-like schedule.

However, the most wonderful part of attending school in the city was traveling back and forth from Makara Beach with Dad. It wasn't so wonderful on frosty winter mornings but did offer us youngsters a chance to check out life in the valley. Dad lighting up his first cigarette of the day as we set off for Wellington was part of our enjoyable ritual. While Dad also smoked cigars and a pipe, he preferred a cigarette while driving.

One of the most exciting events came in 1936, when Dad bought a shiny, six-cylinder Chevrolet. That signaled, for us at least, the end of the Great Depression.

In the morning after dropping all four of us near school, Dad would leave the car near the Royal Tiger Hotel. He parked on a little side street leaving the doors unlocked. Nobody locked any doors in those days and in fact the front door to our Makara home never did have a key. Although our sisters would remain in school and do their homework, Brian and I were out of our school building as soon as the end-of-the-day bell rang. We then had three hours to kill, from 4 p.m. until 7 p.m., when Dad would be ready to drive home from work.

On our car ride back to Makara we would burst into song as we left the city, all of us singing our way home where Mum was waiting with dinner.

Stellamaris, high-spirited as always, led the singing. She had a lovely voice, as did Quita. My sisters knew all the popular songs of the 1930s. Brother Brian hummed along. Our nightly repertoire going home changed from time to time but the Old Irish and Scottish ballads became part of the nooks and crannies of the road. "What about *Shine on Harvest Moon?*" Dad would request. That was Dad's favorite along with a tune he sang called *Ramona*. One moment we would be, *On the Isle of Capri*, and the next, symptomatic of the long trip, *It's a long, long way to Tipperary*, which was reserved for the last stretch of road. We signed off with, the English version of the Maori farewell song, *Now is the Hour*, or if there was time, we might end the trip with *God Save the King*, or even *Auld Lang Syne*. Dad even seemed to manage a little dancing movement with the car on the winding road when we all gave our hearty rendition of *Waltzing Matilda*.

Arguing time among us offspring came after tea (dinner), over the issue of who did which domestic chores. There were three choices: clearing away the table after dinner, washing the dishes, or drying them and stacking them away. Sometimes the girls would be accused of being "lucky dogs" when they were excused from washing or drying because they were cramming for an exam. Homework was an even greater ordeal by gaslight or the flickering candles. Our lengthy day was not unusual. Children all over rural New Zealand had to walk, ride a horse or bike, or otherwise travel long miles back and forth to school.

On a glorious summer's day, rather than wait for Dad, Brian and I would take the tram to Karori and walk the rest of the way home. In this manner we got to know every inch of the gravel road intimately and could count the daily toll of crushed hedgehogs that we believed were trying to hitch a ride home to their ancestral England. The gullies were filled with foxgloves blooming in abundance. The trees at the Duffeys' arched over the road forming a cool tunnel and the branches took on the weirdest of shapes and shadows.

If we waited for Dad to finish work, Brian and I could browse the city in the interim. When the bright new railway station was completed we used it as our waiting room. At the beginning, after the school day at Marist, I would sometimes visit Sister Benignus, at her quarters in St. Mary's Convent. She was a gracious elderly nun, of the Order of Mary, and a great-aunt. I took tea and scones in her lovely parlor, reeking of polish and cleaning fluids. However my religious fervor was sorely tested as I learned that prayer alone didn't necessarily get you through exams.

I sometimes suspected that my mother, who had gone to the Dominican nuns' St. Dominick's academy in Dunedin and was a lifetime member of the *Old Girls' Association,* wanted me, the eldest son, to become a priest. But New Zealand was not Ireland and I had too many diverse interests to be a priest and they included an enthusiasm I shared with my Celtic ancestors for horses.

Most of our family had inherited the old Celtic penchant for horse racing—or at least betting on them. (Uncle Frank loved gambling, bought a racehorse and even crossed the law by doing a spot of bookmaking, which was illegal then.) Gradually I got to know every horse in Makara. My favorite was a palomino, with white mane and tan body. The horse I finally received, temporarily, was Ginger, a big, handsome, red gelding. Pat Smith gave Ginger to us and he became mine, until Geoffrey assumed possession when I got too busy with other pursuits. Ginger was well trained and a lovable creature and I even rode him to a Makara Hall dance one Saturday night.

At Marists, there were the usual school bullies who called Brian and me Huns when they learned that our name was German. Hitler had risen to power in Europe. But Baby Brian and I gave them bare-knuckle Irish responses, quickly ending the name-calling.

Discipline was tough, but so were the kids in the all-male institution. The school had what we referred to as a classroom racetrack. The rules were simple and speed was all-important. The Marist brother in charge of the class was armed with a long, thin, bamboo rod. He used it as a pointer and to give us the right meter for our poetry—and also to tan our backsides when we were accused of some violation of class decorum. The boy to be caned had to run across the room in front of the class. The brother-teacher would, depending on his anger or state of health, get in one good lash with his bamboo cane. It was a sporting way to discipline us and we learned to run close by the brother to avoid the stinging tip of the cane. However if we came too close and made it impossible for the brother to swing the cane, he ordered up a new run.

I ran the gauntlet and it is what I most recall of Marist, besides soccer, free milk and the theatrical performances of our English teacher. Much later when I attended all-male St. Patrick's College, "the old Grey Mother" they called her, caning was administered by a Marist priest who had the title of discipline master and had become an expert in the art. The errant student was made to bend over and receive four or six wallops with a thin, supple, willow cane. The heavy worsted short pants didn't help much, and a new boy who was foolish enough to try to hide a book in his pants to absorb the blows was given double punishment. No one ever got away with cushioning the blow.

Nevertheless Discipline Master Father Maurice Bourke was not without Christian charity. Once I was caned for being late. The second time I was late, I went to Father Bourke, who later became rector of St. Pat's, and suggested that he cane my father instead, explaining that it was he who was late, not I. Then I recounted how we had to travel in from Makara Beach and took the position that I shouldn't be held responsible for my father's running behind schedule. Father Bourke understood and I was never caned again for being late.

One day a new student arrived at Marist. He was an American, whose Catholic father was opening a Coca-Cola plant in New Zealand. We sipped the strange drink and it was quickly condemned as tasting like sheep dip.

Some mornings as we walked from where our father dropped us off, hopping and skipping the last few blocks to Hawkstone Street and school, we would doff our little school caps to Mr. Michael Joseph Savage, the Prime Minister, on his morning walk before going to the nearby Parliament buildings. "Good morning, boys," would be his greeting. Mr. Savage was a gentle person who didn't look at all well. But his Labor Party's election triumph in 1935 had changed all our lives for the better. My mother was ecstatic with the election of Mr. Savage and the implementation of the Labor Party's welfare programs, which redressed many of New Zealand's inequities and brought in social security and free health care. Prime Minister Savage also had parliamentary sessions broadcast over the radio for the first time. As one New Zealand historian noted, "The working class, the Catholics and indeed the Maoris, began to receive a fairer deal."

I was one of the early beneficiaries of the latter when they finally decided that I was all blocked up by infected tonsils and adenoids, and excised them at the Wellington General Hospital. The operation and aftermath were painful and for years I could smell the chloroform which they used to put me to sleep.

Mum reminded us that the Prime Minister was the son of Irish immigrants as was Sir Joseph Ward who had been both Premier and then when they change the title, Prime Minister. And to think, she often said, that the English had tried to restrict the Irish from entering New Zealand as immigrants.

Culturally our Irish heritage was given a lift on St. Patrick's Day. We spent long hours at St. Francis Hall, on Hill Street next to St. Mary's Convent, preparing a whole repertoire of Irish songs for the St. Pat's Day festival that was held at the Wellington Town Hall. Sitting there in the Town Hall surrounded by all the Catholic school kids in Wellington I was shocked, one year, to see Auntie Molly featured on the program. When she sang solo I wanted to hide, as I and the rest of the students had little appreciation for classical singing although she was an accomplished vocalist.

Even as a society identified with macho "mates," New Zealanders relished music. According to an official statistic, in 1901 with a population of only 800,000 there were more than 43,000 pianos in homes around the country. Yet we Diederich kids (the boys) had only pity for a cousin, Richard Farrell, a child prodigy at the piano, who was forced to wear velvet suits and play at the Wellington Opera House. (He was killed in an auto accident in Switzerland at an early age. He did everything young, including dying.)

At Marist Brothers School you were guaranteed to learn more

Irish songs than English poetry. All the same, we had our share of English rhyme from the elderly, theatrical brother-teacher who would wave his bamboo cane dangerously low over our heads in the front row as he literally drummed poetry into us. He had some success. I left the Marists with an enduring appreciation and a full panoply of English poetry. John Masefield's *Sea-Fever* stayed with me, and when I eventually went off to sea I recited it to my sisters who objected to my sailing away: "I must go down to the sea again, to the lonely sea and the sky . . ." Gray's *Elegy in a Country Churchyard* evoked in my mind farmers like George Hawkins: " . . . the ploughman homeward plods his weary way and leaves the world to darkness and to thee . . ." Another poem, which made me think of Makara, was Sir Walter Scott's *The Lay of the Last Minstrel:*

> "Breathes there the man with soul so dead
> Who never to himself hath said,
> This is my own, my native land!
> Whose heart hath ne'er within him burned,
> As home his footsteps he hath turned."

We were taught a love of Empire. Our duty was to King and country. We saw no contradiction in this as members of the conservative Irish branch of the Roman Catholic church that kept Hell's fires well stoked for sinners and English Protestants. The Pope was infallible and so was Mother England. "Home" was on the other side of the world and we studied more about William the Conqueror's 1066 invasion of England and King Harold's taking an arrow in the eye and the bastard King John and the other vicissitudes of English history than about New Zealand.

Our culture was a frigid Anglo-Saxon import. And as supposedly wild colonial youths we were inferior creatures to our counterparts back in our Mother Country.

As if that weren't enough to make you walk with your head under your arm, our Catholicism demanded that we be meek, mild, humble, unpretentious and undemonstrative. Developing an assertive personality was left to nature. Luckily we had plenty of nature at Makara. But there was no disputing the fact that our conformist society of the early 1930s discouraged healthy egos and self-esteem. As knavish jokers ourselves we accepted the foreign jest that New Zealand was the land of millions of sheep, a million and a half of whom believed they were human. To stretch the gibe, hair was uniformly shorn short in much the same manner as sheep's wool. Our bland, somber male fashions of dark, drab woolen suits gave us the same homogeneous look as the domesticated ruminant. We were indeed the sheep of the Empire. We had more *tapus* than the Maoris who were much more original in their dress and behavior. The country got its own respect back by saying nothing good of the "bloody Pommy [effete Englishmen] bastards." However God was still an Englishman and both God and the Devil were part of our everyday lingo, which could be called "Kiwi speech" and which was one thing that we could claim as our own. "God spare the crows you little devils," my father would picturesquely complain in our local argot. "Children are to be seen not heard!"

It was but a short walk from the Marist School to the Parliament buildings. Along the way, on Molesworth Street, there was a Greek-owned fish and chips shop, which, because of its inviting aromas, was difficult to pass. Three pence bought a lot of chips. Then I would run through the Parliament buildings and end up at Aunt Hilda's, whose house at 22 Bolton Street was a lovely old two-story wooden Victorian structure. The banisters leading to the second story shone brightly from daily polishing. Two members of Parliament were lodgers at Aunt Hilda's when they were in town.

Much later I discovered Turnbull Library which had the wonderful atmosphere of one of London's private Pall Mall Clubs which I later had a chance to visit. At the library I spent many a cold evening before a fire looking at picture books and reading early New Zealand history. The librarians were gracious and I couldn't believe so few people took advantage of this wonderful place. I often found myself alone in the library.

As Dad had repeatedly warned, the city was not the countryside where the pleasures of life are free. As tantalizing as Wellington was in the late 1930s I still hung on to Makara, until one day I was offered a job after school. I had had too much time on my hands after school waiting for Dad, and although he preferred that we boys not work, I decided it was time to earn some spending money. In my mind it was extracurricular activity, learning about work and the world of business. (It wasn't then the habit in New Zealand to give children weekly allowances as in some countries.)

It was at the bottom of Bolton Street, in a building called the Kelvin Chambers, that I began an early career as a delivery boy in the city. Bolton Street was on a very steep hill, the steepest in Wellington, which was laced with steep streets. One day I did the Kelvin Chambers grocer a favor by delivering an order to a home at the top of Bolton Street.

This led to my being hired at five shillings a week. Wheeling a bike-load of groceries, mostly vegetables, up the steep Bolton Street hill, and the streets neighboring it, was no fun. So when the chemist (pharmacist) next door needed a delivery boy and an assistant after school and during holidays, and offered me seven shillings a week, I switched jobs.

My predecessor in the job had been addicted to British comic books of the day, Triumph, Champion and Chums, and was fired for misuse of funds. He had taken money out of the cash register to purchase the latest comic books. I inherited not only his job but also a cupboard of comic books he had stored away. Like every youth of that era, I was also a comic book addict but I didn't "tickle the till," as the chemist called unauthorized withdrawals from the cash register.

While serving customers I learned about some of the discreet items stocked by the pharmacist shop. One customer needed some kind of non-prescription article but stammered badly. When he finally managed to blurt out that he wanted to purchase "French letters," I was about to direct him to the post office when the chemist, visibly embarrassed, intervened and from a special drawer slid a packet of condoms as unobtrusively as he could to the poor man.

Every penny I earned I jealously guarded to buy a bicycle. The day I took delivery of that BSA (British Sore Arse, that's what we called the British Small Arms company that manufactured both bicycles and motorbikes as well as rifles and pistols) was one of those unforgettably exciting days of boyhood. I rode my brand-new bike out to Karori and then down Makara Hill. The adventure almost ended in tragedy. Losing control going down Makara Hill I smashed into a cliff and collapsed in a pile. I feared even to look at the bike but when I did it had passed the test. It was hardly scratched.

A later career move took me across the street to a petrol station where I pumped petrol and replenished oil. I wanted a sport coat; it took a long time but I finally saved enough and bought a traditional Harris tweed.

Sometimes because of my after-school jobs I missed my ride with Dad and had to walk home, a long, lonely hike. At the time we youngsters were ritually warned of another danger: lunatics, homicidal maniacs that might escape from the mental hospital at Porirua across the hills. Our society still had much the same primitive view of mentally ill people that prevailed in the Middle Ages when it was thought that they were witches or warlocks possessed by demons.

One evening, returning home on foot from Wellington on a pitch-black night, I heard the crunch of the gravel ahead which meant a person was approaching. As the heavy footsteps got closer I realized the person was walking in the center of the road where the gravel piled up high. That was certainly odd. Suddenly the dark form of a big man brushed by me. "Good evening," I said. The man ignored me—unheard of in our neighborly society. No one ignored anyone at Makara. This encounter was scary. The man must be deaf or worse, I thought! A short while afterward my father and mother arrived in the car looking for me. "A psychopath has fled the mental hospital and is loose in the Makara area. We were worried he might get you," my father said. "Yes!" I told them and jumped in the car. "I just met him." It was he and the following day the poor man was apprehended and returned to the Insane Asylum.

Dad often got us up at dawn during the summer to play tennis prior to our heading off to school. I loved my Slazenger racquet but tennis with Baby Brian was no fun. In fact it was infuriating. He had learned how to slice the ball and force his opponent to run in all directions. Of course that's part of the game but I considered it unsporting and we ended up arguing. Stellamaris and Quita played good classical tennis and excelled in the sport at school. Punished by Baby Brian I lost interest in tennis.

It also upset me that our tennis court attracted Uncle Frank and all his friends to Makara on summer weekends, which meant my mother had to cook Sunday dinner for a score or more of uninvited guests.

(In Mexico decades later I played some racquetball and one time competed against film stars Anthony Quinn and Charles Bronson when they were making a movie [*The Guns of San Sebastian*] on location in Durango in the late 1960s. It was not until I was covering the long summer and fall crisis in Haiti for *TIME* magazine in 1994 that I took up tennis again, at the Montana Hotel in the hills above Port-au-Prince. I then realized how much I enjoyed the game. I wanted to say, "Thanks Dad.")

Because of our myriad school activities and chores, it seemed that the only spare time we had during the worst days of winter was for snatches of reading. Zane Grey's cowboy books were particular favorites in New Zealand, not only for their adventurous plots but possibly because the American author was a friendly visitor; he loved deep-sea fishing in New Zealand's Bay-of-Island in the far north. Later came books by or about T.E. Lawrence— Lawrence of Arabia—a childhood hero, and Count Felix Von Luckner's activities recounted in *The Sea Devil's Fo'c'sle* by Lowell Thomas, who was a great promoter of hero worship. And when we read Emily Bronte's *Wuthering Heights* the sound effects provided by our howling wind outside were all too real.

As good Catholics we would never eat meat on Friday, and on that day it became a custom to take fish and chips home wrapped in newspaper. It was agony spending the automobile trip closeted with the fish and chips without being able to sample that delicious food. We often gave a ride home on a Friday to Frank Monk, a farmer who attended a Worker's Party meeting in Wellington at the end of each month. His presence interrupted our customary singsong and, having spent much of the afternoon eulogizing egalitarianism with comrades at the pub, he was in an argumentative mood. But he would come in for some good-natured kidding from Dad, who would taunt Monk with:

"The working class can kiss my arse for I have the foreman's job at last. Keep the red flag flying."

It was sung to the tune of the Communist International. Monk would hardly notice, being too busy continuing his proletarian arguments, by then mostly to himself.

CHAPTER 20

The World's Best Coach

Our native-born heroes were rugby and cricket players, aviators and aviatrixes and boxers. We were lucky to have one of the latter of our very own; and what was more, he became our personal coach. Uncle Brian McCleary was an exacting coach. He not only taught us boys to box but also track and horsemanship. If he caught us climbing up on the wrong side of a horse, he would reprimand us severely. Nor would he stand for any foolishness when we were in training.

He himself was a remarkable all-around sportsman. He had become New Zealand's national amateur heavyweight boxing champion in 1920, and the following year he not only successfully defended his amateur title but turned pro, becoming our country's heavyweight professional champion. Thus Uncle Brian was a true celebrity in our midst. He finally lost the pro boxing crown to Tom "Hard Rock" Heeney in an epic bout.

It was therefore Heeney from Gisborne—though it could well have been Brian McCleary—who became the first New Zealander to fight for the world heavyweight championship. The bout was against the American Gene Tunney in 1928. Heeney lost by decision.

"Technically, he [Brian McCleary] was one of the best equipped big men the sport has produced," wrote Brian O'Brien in his book, *Kiwis with Gloves On*.

Furthermore, as a footballer (rugby player) our Uncle Brian was recalled as a tough, nuggety forward, strong on the tackle and vigorous on the loose. He played for the champion Marist team in

Christchurch after returning from Europe at the end of World War I. It was then that he met Dad, and later they moved to Culverden and Brian played representative rugby with Dad who was captain of the Canterbury team.

In 1924 Brian was chosen to play as a member of the National team, the All Blacks. The All Blacks were known at years as the "Invincibles." They toured Australia, Britain and Canada and even played a game in California, winning every match on their tour. And Uncle Brian played in every game.

Dad, because he was either too busy or perhaps believed Uncle Brian was a better teacher, left the coaching to him. Uncle Brian was indeed an exacting tutor. In boxing training he would clip your ear with a fast left hook if you didn't do as he instructed. There was no questioning of his method. He was right and you followed. He prepared Baby Brian, Geoffrey and me for the ring. Geoffrey won the St. Patrick's College (the boarding college at Silverstream) heavyweight boxing championship and I won St. Patrick's College heavyweight championship in 1941—all thanks to Uncle Brian. But I detested boxing as a sport; two men smashing each other's brains out repelled me. Still and all, we had the best trainer and coach any boy could dream of.

Young Brian, or Baby Brian, didn't take kindly to being bashed around in the ring. By contrast, as a dazzled sportswriter noted, in the *Evening Post* on one occasion, Geoffrey knocked out one of his opponents with a powerful punch that sent the other pugilist completely out of the ring. It was the highlight of the evening's boxing card. The sportswriter added that Geoffrey embodied one of the best heavyweight physiques ever seen in New Zealand, declaring: "Aged 17, he should grow into a full-fledged heavyweight, as he has the height, reach, shoulders and chest of the champion with not too much weight in the legs to impede speed of movement. That he should show such ringcraft is not surprising in view of uncle Brian McCleary's coaching. Tom Heeney once stated that Brian McCleary was one of the most scientific boxers he met whether in New Zealand or overseas."

Indeed Uncle Brian's room, in our maternal grandparents' house next door at Makara, was a museum of awards, decorations and citations. The walls were covered with rugby photos and as young children we proudly wore his collection of small, tasseled championship caps.

Among the mementos was a framed portrait of a North American Indian on horseback before a teepee. It was a Blackfoot Indian chief whom Uncle Brian had befriended during his tour of Canada—Chief Buffalo Child Long Lance, whose books about his tribe gave us a deeper understanding of the traditions of the North American Indians. The most recent photographs on the wall were of a bearded Uncle Brian prospecting for gold in the South Island. The venture was unprofitable, he used to say, but pleasurable.

Not of a sporting nature was Punch, a white bull terrier that Uncle Brian brought home. Punch was a very nasty dog and when he almost took a piece out of Stellamaris we kept away from him. One day Punch attacked my dog, Astor, and almost ripped the little cocker to pieces. When we finally separated them it appeared that little Astor was done for, as he went into a fit. Auntie Madge saved Astor by crushing some aspirin in milk and pouring it down the dog's throat. The bull terrier finally killed some sheep and had to be put away—shot! It was a farming law that once a dog kills a sheep he must pay the price with his or her life. We were not sad to see Punch go.

In all his exploits Uncle Brian, like most "Kiwis," was self-effacing and not even prone to self-expression. New Zealanders were not supposed to boast. Humility and modesty were virtues to be encouraged. When by contrast the famous New Zealand aviatrix Jean Batten became the first woman to fly the Tasman Sea to Australia, and talked only of herself giving no credit to anyone else not even her mechanics, she was branded an upstart and a terrible "skite." Skite was the Kiwi word for one who brags or boasts.

CHAPTER 21

An Empire of Heroes

The main attraction in Wellington was the Saturday afternoon movies, which required a six-pence entrance fee. There were weekly serials at the Deluxe Cinema such as *Bulldog Drummond of Scotland Yard*, and even a wonderful New Zealand-made movie, the name of which I have forgotten but whose vivid scenes of the countryside were so beautifully filmed that I can still see them.

Our celluloid entertainment fare was filled with romance of the Empire, strong and benevolent defender of the weak! One of the first movies I ever saw was *Sanders of the River* (1935) with the American black actor Paul Robeson as Bosambo singing praise of the British colonial officer Sanders. This film, like the rest—such as *Lives of a Bengal Lancer*, *Trader Horn*, *Clive of India*, *Rhodes of Africa*, *Stanley and Livingstone*, *The Four Feathers*, *Gunga Din* and *The Lost Patrol*—were at heart jingoistic brainwashing. We children of course didn't realize it at the time. Most of these black-and-white flicks, many of which were directed by the Hungarian Zoltan Korda, brother of the more famed director Alexander Korda, presented such a rosy and powerful view of the British Empire that when we saw a scarlet tunic it gave us a feeling of well-being, justice and righteousness.

After viewing one of these flattering pro-Empire movies the audience would stand ramrod straight and some even sang *God Save the King*, which was played before and after each film showing and at most other public and even some private functions.

We were of course all loyal sons of the Empire. Neither we nor anyone that we knew questioned the jingoism of those movies.

They made life so simple. Years before Rudyard Kipling's poem
Gunga Din was made into a film, I decided like any adventurous
son of the Empire that I wanted to enter the Imperial British Army
and serve on the North-West Frontier of India. Kipling was my
symbolic recruiting officer when he wrote:

> "Though I've belted you and flayed you
> By the living Gawd that made you
> You're a better man that I am, *Gunga Din!*"

Our other heroes were also imported along with our Christmas dinner menu of roast beef and plum puddings. Those heroes
or rather the Empire's heroes were cloaked in the highest values of
man and devoted to King and Country (England). Chivalry was
alive and well in the Empire! The only New Zealand addition to
our Christmas dinner were the small, silver New Zealand three-
penny pieces that Mum hid in our plum pudding.

Among our heroes were also the early British Antarctic explor-
ers and aviators. The self-sacrifice of Captain Oats during the ill-
fated expedition led by Robert Falcon Scott to the South Pole caught
the imagination of us all. Oat's self abnegation was what the Empire expected. Frostbitten in both feet, Capt. Lawrence Oats, in
order to give his food ration to his companions, crawled out of his
expedition's tent into a terrible blizzard, telling his fellow explor-
ers, "I may be some time." (Ironically they were only 29 miles
from a food depot on their tragic return from the Pole to which
they had already been beaten by the Norwegian explorer Ronald
Amundsen.)

Oats' sacrifice didn't save his companions who made only a
few more miles before they too died in the blizzard. Still, Captain
Oats of the 6th Inniskilling Dragoons made us all proud to be
part of the Empire. It was in the heroic tradition, the right stuff.
Oats was, as the leader of the expedition, Robert Falcon Scott wrote
before he also died to be interred in a snowy grave in Antarctica, "a
brave man and an English gentleman."

And hadn't we all read the theme in *A Tale of Two Cities* by

Charles Dickens about the ultimate sacrifice, in which Carton takes
the place of Darnay and goes to the guillotine in his stead? I saw
the film and became much more interested in this English writer.
I could recite Dickens' ending of that book: "It is a far, far better
thing that I do, than I have ever done . . ."

In short, our childhood years were an era inspired by the concept of heroes, real or imagined. Even Dick Turpin, the English
highwayman who was featured in an early movie, was a good bad
guy, as was Robin Hood. We had little idea of the real world out
there; it was too far away (although the cinema newsreels gave us a
hint). And I always remember that when Big Black Jim Martin
tried to tell us how the real world was, we couldn't believe him. It
couldn't be as he pictured it, which was just too unbelievable, too
cruel.

In sum we were shown only one side of the cosmic coin. After
World War II, when I arrived in England for the first time to further my education, I, a New Zealander, found it both familiar and
exhilarating. Everything I saw both delighted me and gave me the
feeling that I had been there before. In a sense I had, in poems and
literature.

Our Marist lay brothers and priests who taught me at lower
school and college (as well as pretty Miss Sherm at Makara School)
had done a good job even though, strangely enough, few of them
were English. The sights and sounds of England lifted my heart
and spirit. I was delighted with what I saw. I was home at last!

CHAPTER 22

Down With the Empire!

It was a long rail trip. Previously I had gone several times alone by train from Wellington to Palmerston North to stay with Grandpa Diederich and to work in his furniture factory. The "Diederich & Sons" sign on Main Street was visible from the train, and only a short walk from the railway station. However, this trip was much longer—to the town of Hawera, in the Taranaki, not far from New Plymouth, three quarters of the way up the North Island. I was ten and going to spend my school holidays with cousins Jack, Paddy and Denis Scanlon. They were sons of our great—grandfather's brother Michael. Theirs was a lovely dairy farm and eighty cows were milked by machine. The paddocks were rich in clover and the view was of the almost perfect, snowcapped cone of Mount Egmont (8,260 ft).

Paddy Scanlon was at the Hawera station to meet me in a Model-A Ford coupe. Their farmhouse was big, sprawling and untidy as there was no woman in the house. It was also a sort of halfway house for newly arrived Irish immigrants from County Kerry, as the Scanlons had once been. The newcomers were assured free shelter and food for as long as they wished before moving on to a job. They were part of the ever-growing Irish Diaspora.

It was rustic farm living. The night before I arrived, a mare had died giving birth and they didn't think the foal would live. I pleaded to take care of it and fed Mary, which we named the female foal, with a bottle of cow's milk several times a day. Mary survived and became a virtual house pet in those early days. Mary eventually grew into a huge workhorse.

The great event was hauling the milk from eighty cows to the cheese factory. Paddy allowed me to drive the six-horse team pulling the wagon filled with 25-gallon milk drums. We would return from the factory with the drums filled with whey, the awful-smelling residue from the process of making cheese, which was fed to the Scanlons' pigs. Besides the dairy they had a considerable pig farm. We ate home-cured bacon every morning for breakfast.

The first time we returned to the farm from the cheese factory, Paddy instructed me to straighten up the pig troughs. The pigsty was covered with black, slimy mud and filled with excited porkers that knew their lunch was about to be served. I quickly obeyed, jumping down into the muck.

I was bending over trying to fix a trough when I was hit by a great wave. It was akin to my tidal wave nightmare, but the sea was a great distance from the farm and I soon realized its source: 25 gallons of stinking whey. Pigs were suddenly all over me. One was frantically sucking at my whey-wet shirt. Although I had been having a hard time understanding the Scanlons' heavy Irish brogue, there was no mistaking Paddy's glee. Helpless with laughter, he thrashed his side with his cap at the sight of me covered by muck and stampeding pigs in search of their whey lunch. I managed to scramble out of the way just as Paddy, still hysterical, readied the second shower. They didn't catch me in the pig trough again.

Irish humor was special and I was learning the hard way. "The Great Gaels of Ireland are the men that God made mad; for all their wars are merry, and all their songs are sad," wrote British author G.K. Chesterton. That day I agreed with the British poet.

Another day the Scanlons handed me the bridle to a big Irish draft horse (no Scottish mongrels for them). "Go fetch that horse in that paddock, laddy," said Jack, the eldest and the boss. The big mare had a little foal beside her and as I got close she reared up. A ton of muscular horseflesh was poised on its huge rear legs above me with its ears pinned back against its head. I knew I had to run and I ran for my life, to the roar of laughter of both Jack and Paddy. Reaching the barbed corral fence with the sound of pounding hoofs in my ears, I dived through it just in time to escape the big mare's huge hoofs. She was so close that I felt her steaming, snorting nostrils on my neck. In my dive a barbed wire tore a piece of my scalp, but even my bleeding didn't spoil my cousins' joke. It was the subtle Irish way of teaching me that only a fool approaches a mare when it has a foal.

I learned their language and more Irish songs, and then one day, naive youngster that I was, I got my first lesson in world politics.

Two cousins from the South Island whose father was in the police force joined us. On Friday nights we were permitted to go to the movies in Hawera, a neat little town. But, as I did until I left home, I would not go out at night without first asking permission. Paddy and Denis usually relented and let me go. An elder boy was allowed to drive the Ford, if Paddy or Denis didn't go along. The town was prim and pretty and all lighted up on Friday nights and the stores stayed open late to allow the area's farmers and their families to shop.

It was the summer holidays following Christmas. The Model A was parked before a grocery store and the storekeeper recognized the Scanlon car. He handed me a big calendar with the ritual portrait of King George V and Queen Mary on it. The King looked splendid in his scarlet military uniform. "Take it home, lad, it will lighten up the year for all of you." He was a Pommy. I could tell by his accent.

The next morning, after milking, I tidied up the house as much as possible and nailed the calendar to the kitchen wall. The King and Queen dominated the whole room, as in so many households in my very English homeland of New Zealand.

I was feeding Mary her bottle at the other side of the house. In fact, though she had grown into a strong little foal, Mary liked to take her bottle in the house. Suddenly the most terrible shrieking shattered the morning calm. I thought an accident had happened. I rushed across the living room toward the kitchen with Mary clattering and sliding behind me on the wooden floor. I caught some thick Irish-brogue words of damnation but I didn't need to understand the words. In the kitchen I found Denis, his face distended dangerously red and on the point of apoplexy, with the calendar twisted in his hands strangling His Majesty and the Queen. I was horrified. Only when he began to rip the calendar to shreds and then literally stamp on the remnants did I realize that Denis was clearly not a loyal subject of the King of England. His usually jolly face still distorted in anger, he stomped off but not before pointing a finger at me and declaring: "Understand that they are bloody murderers, murderers of your kin . . ."

It was Paddy and Jack who later took the time to explain that Black-and-Tan meant not just a mixture of Guinness and beer. The Black-and-Tans Paddy said were a barbaric paramilitary force recruited in England, mostly veterans of the Great War (1914-18), who wore black police tunics and tan army trousers and who were used by the Crown to crush the Irish independence movement. Some of my relatives I was told had been members of the Sinn Fein and Irish Republican Brotherhood—IRA—and some had been killed by the British.

Paddy wasn't talking only to me. It was as if he was talking to all Irishmen in New Zealand "Didn't you know that the great Irishman, Roger Casement, had landed in Tralee Bay at Banna Strand—not far from your family's farms—in April 1916 on a Maundy Thursday? Didn't you know that the British had captured him and hanged him? He landed at Banna Strand . . . !"

Two young recent Irish immigrants who were staying at the house had rushed in to see what the agitated discussion was all about. Hearing Paddy talking about Casement and Banna Strand, they did what the Irish do best and burst into song—the *Ballad of Lonely Banna Strand*. The lyrics recall the 20,000 German rifles that Casement was bringing to help the Irish rise up and throw off the British yoke, and how Casement washed up on Banna Strand only to be seized by the British. Ironically Sir Roger had been a Protestant from County Antrim, but his fellow Irish of the Roman faith considered him a great man nevertheless and the Scanlons maintained that he had died a Catholic anyway. Hanged by the Crown.

There was another ditty my cousins sang:

"We're off to Dublin with the green on green, our helmets
glistening in the sun; and the Tans they run, like lightning
from, the rattle of a Thompson gun . . ."

That whole experience involving Paddy, Jack and Denis Scanlon
was tough psychological stuff for me. It was like learning about a
death in the family. The Empire that was all greatness was being
questioned by my own relatives—were they the enemy? I tried not
to think too much about it. It was confusing. As they were always
making me the butt of a joke maybe this story of Mr. Casement
was all a joke. But they had sown the seed of doubt and the Empire was never again quite the same, not as morally unquestionable
as I had thought it had been, after that summer in Taranaki.

Although I was too young to realize the entire political signifi-
cance of the long, ongoing struggle of the Irish, I now knew that
they—and part of me—were second-class citizens, subordinate to
the English Protestants. Was it such a terrible thing I had done to
the Scanlons, I thought, by putting up the King and Queen in
their house?

For years, however, I kept wondering why my Irish cousins
chose to live in the British Empire under the Union Jack flag. As if
to respond to my question they didn't remain in New Zealand but
eventually sold their farm and returned to live out their lives in the
Irish Republic, in Tralee.

I shared the story of hanging their Majesties in the Scanlons'
home with Stellamaris, and one day when she and I went to the
movies together, she said, "Let's not stand to *God Save the King.*" It
was the new King, George VI. We said it would be an act of soli-
darity with our Irish forebears who had fought the English. But at
the last minute we melted and stood up.

CHAPTER 23

Makara Goes to War

In the summer of 1936 we toured the North Island of New Zealand. Uncle Brian and Dad insisted that we children see our country first, "in case you decide one day to go overseas," they said. How right they were. It was the most wonderful trip.

We had Uncle Frank's new Pontiac and a trailer. We visited Rotorua and had our own thermal bath on the banks of Lake Taupo. The family prevented me from tickling streams teeming with rainbow trout. The world-famous Waitomo glowworm caves were another strange world, with a million lights aglow in the dark. When we reached The Mount (actually Mt. Maunganui) at Tauranga in the Bay of Plenty, the powdery sand beaches at its base were heaven. The weather was warmer than I had ever experienced and for days we lived in a small lodge and I helped the man with the donkey concession, selling rides along the beaches.

With indigenous birds serenading us we traveled through cool mountains of a profusion of ferns and unspoiled native bush. We sang our hearts out to the geysers, boiling mud pools in the thermally active regions. We discovered all the wonders of our enchanting land and it was just in time. The world as we knew it was about blow up like a Rotorua geyser.

Then almost too quickly, it was 1939 and I was spending a few days in Palmerston North with my Diederich grandparents. Sitting next to the radio, reading a book on the use of guerrilla tactics during the Boer War (1899)—the first war to which New Zealand had sent her soldiers—I suddenly heard the BBC interrupt a musical program. "This is London calling, here is news." It was news that was to alter much of our lives, and it was the beginning of the end of life as we had lived it at Makara. Hitler had just invaded Poland.

Adolf Hitler was taking on the world. Grandfather Diederich was visibly upset. He was as adamantly opposed to "that crazy man Hitler" as any other New Zealander. His reactions were those of a New Zealander, not a native-born German. The rest of our family never thought of Grandfather Diederich as an "enemy alien." In fact few New Zealanders who knew him did.

To be sure, he must have had some difficult moments during the First World War (1914-18) when patriotic fervor in New Zealand became violent.

The German population in New Zealand was minuscule. Yet it might be said that New Zealanders, occupying the outer edges of the Empire, were more rabidly patriotic than the British. At one point during World War I, some overheated patriots went on an anti-German hunt in Wanganui, a town north of Palmerston North, where Grandpa and Nana Diederich had spent their bicycle honeymoon. The mob smashed a butcher shop owned by a German and then the windows of the Hallenstein Brothers' clothing store and those of the old Dresden Piano Company. The rioters were soon reminded by then-Prime Minister William Massey that smashing windows had not hurt the German war effort but had hurt the British insurance companies that were required to pay for the damage.

The hysteria had not touched Grandpa; still he was careful enough to use the business name of "B. Smith" in place of his own during the Great World War. It was not a permanent name change, as some had carried out. Many of the German-sounding names involved were in fact those of Jewish families. Schneideman Brothers for example felt obliged to advertise the fact that they came, not from Germany, but from Riga in Russia and were soon promoting themselves as "The Empire Tailors."

By the time World War II erupted, the name "Diederich & Sons" was again plainly displayed over my grandfather's furniture store on Palmerston North's Main Street. Prime Minister Savage, perhaps mindful of the anti-German riots that occurred during World War I, addressing the nation on Sept. 5, 1939, made a distinction between Nazis and the German people: "None of us has any hatred of the German people. We are fighting a doctrine that springs from a contempt of human nature."

Gallipoli and the World War I trenches of France had devastated a whole generation of young New Zealanders, and now the slaughter of war was to happen again. Grandpa Diederich was now to lose his most successful son, Uncle Roy, to the Axis guns of World War II. New Zealanders were patriotic to the Crown. Most didn't question their duty and enlisted. Some were driven, like Uncle Roy, by their beliefs. (Our evening concerts going home with Dad changed to include the over-optimistic, *We're gonna hang out our washing on the Siegfried Line.*)

As for me, by then growing into adolescence, I had decided I would not miss this Second World War. It was more than just duty. On my return to Wellington from Palmerston North, I learned that the young fellow with whom I worked after school and on Saturdays at the petrol station opposite the Kelvin Chambers, and who was a member of the Army's territorials—they were part of the Army reserve and wore snappy, trim, blue-and-red dress uniforms—had reported for duty. I had once beaten him in a fistfight behind the petrol pumps and believed I could do as well as he in the Army.

I thereupon tried to enlist but my effort was hardly a resounding success. The leathery recruiting sergeant who happened to know my father and who checked my age was kind enough, but when he turned me down I felt he should not have discriminated against me because of my youth.

However, the manager of the petrol station had been a wireless officer aboard a merchant ship, and he suggested that the Navy might be a better place for me than the Army. He began to teach me Morse code. The practicing of dots and dashes was fun but my tutor's stories of sailing around the world were more interesting.

I had bought my first camera around this time, a little Kodak Brownie, and saved all the money I could to buy film and have my pictures developed at the chemist's. When the First Echelon of New Zealand soldiers embarked for North Africa on the big British and Canadian luxury liners that had been converted into troop ships, I was there on the docks recording for history their departure. It was an emotional scene, those young fresh-faced soldiers, and mostly farmers, waving goodbye from the railings of the big, gray troopships.

A police officer stopped me; I did not consider it an arrest. He took my name, and sized me up as a spy in short pants. "What's your name, laddy?" he asked, "Age?" "You're big for 13. But you could be working for the enemy. You know you shouldn't be taking these pictures of the troops leaving. This is a restricted area. Diederich? Isn't that German?" "It's New Zealand," was my impertinent reply. "Where does your father work?" The policeman let me go with his big wagging finger in my face. Later he had a beer with Dad and the matter was forgotten by all but me.

The departures of the troops of the First and then the Second Echelons for North Africa were hardly cloaked in secrecy. Wellingtonians, from the vantage point of their homes or offices, could easily take photos of the troop ships leaving. The whole of Wellington watched as the big ships moved out into the harbor. The soldiers climbed to the highest point to wave goodbye to the City. I had even thought of stowing away on one of them and I could have done so without any trouble. But I didn't want to upset my parents.

My journalism career had already begun with my interest in photography. In 1940 I assigned myself to cover the triumphant return of our country's warship *H.M.S. Achilles* from winning (for us) the Battle of the River Plate off Montevideo, Uruguay, in which the Germans were forced to scuttle their pocket battleship, the *Graf Spee*. Among my other projects was the Centennial Eucharistic Congress held on the grounds of St. Patrick's College, by then my new school. The most depressing assignment I gave myself was covering the funeral of Prime Minister Savage.

Despite the fact that in 1939 I was on the verge of entering college at venerable St. Pat's—the Marists' first overseas secondary school, opened in 1885—my younger brother Brian and I had begun selling the *Evening Post*, Wellington's leading newspaper. I was to learn the nuts and bolts of the newspaper business in the streets of Wellington. It was fun. We would pick up our supply of newspapers at the *Post's* printing plant under the paper's editorial offices on Willis Street. I loved the smell of the ink and the roar of the big presses as they rolled off the evening edition.

We paperboys, as we were called, had our own special sales cry, a high-pitched yodel: "Evening paper!" The *Post* cost two pence each and lots of customers would give us the small three-penny piece and let us keep the big copper penny change. We had designated corners. Mine was at the bottom of Plimmer Steps, and Baby Brian's was on another corner farther down Lampton Quay.

On a portable sidewalk board provided by the newspaper we affixed the screaming headline of the day to entice buyers. With our newspapers under one arm we learned to fold a copy with the other hand, present it to the buyer, receive payment and give change in one swift manoeuver. The service had to be fast and efficient. To each customer you said, "Tar," slang for thank you. (Women rarely bought the newspaper.)

There was a marvelous bakery shop not far from my sales post and I often spent my night's profit on a bun or cake.

Tired of standing, stamping in the cold, and jingling the big brown coppers in my pocket I decided to create my own sales route. Brian did the same. We used to enter the pubs and sell our papers—tipping was always better in the pubs—and then pick up a piece of counter-lunch, usually chunks of stale cheese. I would also go over to the Army headquarters and stroll down the corridors selling the paper, all the while marveling at the possibilities if I had been a spy. I was never stopped. The long corridors were interesting and I would enter offices and offer the *Evening Post* to military clerks and officers seated behind desks piled with official papers. We usually had sold our quota of newspapers by the time Dad picked us up for our drive home to Makara. (The paper didn't publish on Sundays).

Much more lucrative than the *Evening Post* however was the *Sports Post*. It was fun and more profitable selling the sports paper so I quit the daily. The *Sports Post* was the most popular weekly and it came out early Saturday evening just as the pubs were closing. The *Sports Post* sold for three pence and was our sporting bible of the week. No sooner had we moved out with our bundle of papers under our arms than the selling began. We would jump on a tram and sell out and then run back to the paper's delivery platform for more issues. All New Zealanders wanted to read the day's rugby, cricket and hockey scores. I myself couldn't wait to devour the stories when our own teams would appear in print. The sports lovers, flushed with beer, were quite generous.

The milk bar, a new institution that sold milkshakes, ice cream and tomato soup, had just come to town, putting greater pressure on my earnings. Brian had more discipline and saved his money. "Shylock" I called him.

In my search for a still more lucrative paper route, and also for a way to contribute to the war effort, I found a gem. When the *Second Echelon* prepared to depart for the Middle East I decided the troops would need some reading material, so I purchased a couple of dozen issues of Wellington's more spicy publications, *Truth* and *The News of the World*. Weekly scandal sheets Mum called them. I went aboard the big troopships and left my pile of newspapers with the quartermaster on duty at the head of the main gangplank, and told him they were six pence each, double the normal sales price. Then I would wander over these marvels of the sea. They were incredibly big converted passenger ships. They still had their elaborate salons, grand staircases, glittering brass and highly polished woodwork, and were still adorned with their glorious fixtures.

There was the four-funnel *Aquitania* and *The Andes*, as well as the Canadian Pacific ships such as, ironically, the *Empress of Japan*. The sailors were extremely honest; the money was always there waiting for me when I left the ship enjoying the fact that my profit margin was the best yet.

I developed an interest in the world and began a foreign-coin collection, asking sailors to swap coins. They would look on their shelves and hand me old coins from Japan, China, Java and the rest of the world. In no time I had a sizable numismatic trove. These were not stereotypical sailors, said to be hell-raisers and drunks. I found them to be the opposite. But St. Pat's cut short my newspaper career. Meanwhile the war was becoming serious for us far-off New Zealanders. Yet it couldn't dampen our nation's Centennial Exhibition which opened in Wellington in November 1939 and continued through April 1940. I was a frequent visitor examining the government's exhibits, which indicated to us that we were advancing into a new world in which the marvels of technology would reign. The visit usually ended in the Playland amusement park where Uncle Frank had a shooting gallery.

*   *   *

When our cousin, Rev. Father Des Scanlon, came home on leave from four years as a New Zealand Marist missionary in the Solomon Islands (then a British protectorate) he stayed with us at Makara and I went to the Centennial Exhibition with him. He had been ordained a priest in 1935, at age of 27. Soon afterwards he was sent to the Solomons. He was a wonderful person and an excellent amateur photographer. His photo albums of life on the Solomon Islands, north of New Guinea, were themselves an extraordinary exhibition. He told us of his adventures with the mountain people who still fancied "long pig" —cannibalism. But his greatest adventure was yet to come.

Cousin Des returned to his mission headquarters at Visale on the island of Guadalcanal saying he would see us again on his next vacation in four years.

It was during Easter, 1927, while lost hiking across the alpine wilderness of the rugged Tararua mountain range with Uncle Roy, that Des had made a vow to devote his life to the missions in the Pacific islands if he and Uncle Roy survived. His prayers were answered. They survived and he kept his promise.

Being lost in the Tararus, made headlines. Grandpa Diederich organized search parties, as did the hiking groups. One only has to look up at this formidable mountain range, visible from Wellington, to realize how easy it must have been to get lost there. The Maoris considered this wilderness sacred, a place of the gods.

Uncle Roy was a law student at Victoria College and cousin Des was attending St. Patrick's College in Wellington when they tackled the mighty Tararua range. It was during a severe storm on their second day that they lost their bearings on the northern end of the range. The storm forced them to seek shelter in a trench of tussocks, which provided some relief from the wind but not the rain. At night they sang to keep warm and after several days their food supplies began to run out. They scooped up water from holes the deer's footprints left in the ground. When the weather abated somewhat, they set off with swollen feet, feeling weak and dizzy. In the deep mist they climbed the wrong mountain ridge. The storm returned, thrashing the mountains, and they were forced to take shelter under a rock. In spite of their weakened and precarious situation, Uncle Roy kept a diary throughout. "Sunday's meal was onion plus sugar, Monday's onion plus pepper," Roy detailed their dwindling supplies, while trapped on the northern peaks of the Tararua.

The notations in his diary are matter-of-fact: "Anzac Day was the worst day of the trip. Heavy rains in the morning, blankets soaked, very uncomfortable . . . made several trips about 50 yards down the valley for water but as time passed found ourselves getting lazy and weaker so got water from drips from rock onto plate . . . position now uncomfortable due to cramp and numbness of feet . . . at times had only to shut eyes to get vivid mental images, bright lights, etc. —Belloc, Prince of Wales, Cathedral, etc . . . . On Saturday night sleep broken by deer ripping off cape over our heads, found footprints in the morning—at times we imagined we heard voices in the valley below—wondered if search parties out, if so concluded that by now they would have given up—both anxious for our people otherwise in no way 'windy' (scared.)

"On Anzac Day read two novels to Des who is anxious to get rid of them in case we should be found dead beside them! —found later that wind had brought them back . . . determined that when mist cleared we would travel back to the forks and pick up the right track . . . rather disgusted that I was spending my annual leave in this manner." Of the night sounds Roy wrote, "Was the occasional mournful calling of the deer." Roy describes the mountains as full of deer and, "we saw great herds of them."

Following Anzac Day, bruised and weakened by hunger, the pair quit their rock shelter and followed a creek down to Avalanche Flats. Steep, moss-covered cliffs proved a daunting obstacle course. Des, at one point, lost his grip and tumbled some 20 feet, losing two teeth when his head banged against a rock. When they finally reached Avalanche Flats they found a cache of food left there purposely by one of the twelve search parties. Roy records: Had a meal of bread, tinned meat and condensed milk, which was A1."

The next morning, after a night's rest, they made their way over Deception Ridge and down the Ohua track to the town of Levin, where they received a civic reception and were hailed for their "pluck and endurance." Their miraculous survival was front-page news through the country. The *New Zealand Freelance,* a pictorial weekly, ran a full page of photos that the pair had taken during their trek. The *Freelance* reported:

"Perhaps no peril so stirs the imagination as the thought of a wreck at sea or wandering lost in the mountains. People may die in a hundred unromantic ways and their friends and near neighbor's mourn. Tragedies occur and accidents happen, and the public sympathy is momentarily aroused. But there is a strange, gripping romance about the fight for life on a trackless mountain.

When Roy Diederich and Desmond Scanlon set out before Easter to tramp across the Tararuas from Levin to Masterton they had a limited circle of personal friends. When they emerged from the mountain mist 14 days later, alive and well, they found themselves welcomed like national heroes.

They had become celebrities." The *Freelance* went on to say that their survival "has also proved the endurance and courage, the coolness of the young New Zealander in a crisis."

According to Chris Maclean in his excellent book *Tararua: The Story of a Mountain Range,* "The Diederich-Scanlon search had a far-reaching influence on the Tararua tramping (hiking) community. Before Easter 1927 few trampers were familiar with the northern part of the range, but a fortnight's intensive searching had introduced many people to new country. Twelve search parties had been involved . . ." In sum the outcome was that the ignorance of the terrain and the absence of tracks (trails), brought about the formation of a new tramping club and the creation of a track. The longer-term effect of the Diederich-Scanlon search opened up the whole of the northern part of the mountains, and it also changed the way tramping was organized.

A testament to the ruggedness of the terrain, during the Second World War the New Zealand army's elite School of Bush and Mountain Warfare used the Tararuas as a training group and some 41 U.S. Marine officers were trained there in jungle warfare before being sent to fight elsewhere in the Pacific.

Des went on to the Greenmeadows Seminary in Napier determined to keep his vow. Uncle Roy continued to captain the New Zealand University rugby team. One of the thrills when I was young was to watch Uncle Roy play rugby at university. He went on to join the staff of the Public Trust Office in 1928 and in 1938 left New Zealand to take up the position of assistant attorney general in the Fiji Islands. Later while there he became a magistrate and coached the Fijian rugby team to victory. The Fijians preferred to play without footware. We were delighted when Roy returned on his first leave from Fiji and shared some vivid stories about Fiji still under British rule. Uncle Roy was my early role model.

(It was in 1944 that Uncle Roy decided at the end of another Fiji leave to enlist in the army for active service as a trooper and went overseas to fight with the New Zealanders in the 8th army in Italy. Even though he held an army commission in Fiji he enlisted as a simple soldier and when asked during a training camp session what he did in civil life he went into an amusing detailed story about making bottle tops.

His correspondence as the Allies moved up through Italy reflected a growing spirituality and he devoted a great deal of space to describing the churches and sanctuaries of Italy.

After surviving most of the horrors of the Italian campaign, on almost the last day of the war, as Uncle Roy and his fellow troopers moved over a river in Northern Italy, German mortar shells rained down on them. Uncle Roy was killed.

His obituary in the *Evening Post* cited him as "One of the most outstanding men of Victoria University in the late twenties and early thirties." The article continued: "Trooper Diederich entered Varsity in 1925 and was capped LL.B in 1930. He took part in all student actives and was president of the students' association in 1932.

"Last Saturday all teams of the Victoria University Club played in white armbands in respect to his memory, and a contemporary remarked at Wakefield Park: 'He had everything—ability, charm and thoughtfulness and he was a great fellow.'"

As I was somewhere in the Pacific at the time on a U.S.ship, it was months before I learned of Uncle Roy's death. I learned then how sad and life changing it is to loose one's mentor.

*   *   *

On March 11, 1941, mum, then 41, surprised us by giving birth to the fourth boy in the family and he was proudly named Patrick. We rejoiced at now being half a dozen kids.

One afternoon, having returned to Makara after seeing a Holly-wood movie on the life of Jessie James, I was looking over the brown hills from our front window. I was struck by a sudden sense of cold realism, the realization that life was not a game, that the gunslingers of the Old West (in the United States) were actually plain murderers, killers, who had been glorified beyond recognition. What was more I suddenly felt I was drowning in claustrophobia. I knew then that I had outgrown both my childhood dreams and Makara. It was like an adolescent embarrassingly shedding the toys of childhood, discard-ing the place of early dreams. It was also the realization that my roots had hit bedrock at Makara. The moaning wind no longer played on the fantasies of my mind. Zane Grey's *Riders of the Purple Sage* had vanished into the morning mist.

The barren hills of Makara with their endless sheep paths go-ing nowhere in particular evoke only sadness now. The area's isolated beaches and bays appeared then to beckon only the occasional stranger.

It all ended for us children when Makara no longer held any secrets or promises of adventure. Its bleakness began to close in with a suffocating sameness and boredom. As Nietzsche put it: "For thinking and all sensitive spirits, boredom is that disagreeable 'windless calm' of the soul that precedes a happy voyage and cheerful winds . . ." We refused to cohabit with the beast of boredom. It failed to enslave us as it had the farmers of the valley and the fishermen around the bay. But it left its mark.

In 1941-on December 7—Japan carried out a devastating attack on Pearl Harbor in the Hawaiian Islands. New Zealand reaction to Pearl Harbor was one of muted surprise but which also welcomed the news that the United States was finally entering the war officially and on all fronts. The real shock for us was the rapid advance of the Japanese troops, like the proverbial tidal wave of those childhood nightmares, into Southeast Asia, plus the sinking of two British battleships and the fall of Singapore. We had never dreamed that such a collapse would be possible.

Singapore was guarding us—the supposedly invincible British colonial Gibraltar of the Pacific. "It would stop the Japs dead," everyone had bragged.(Four years later I was ultimately to end my war service in Singapore, witnessing the humiliating Japanese surrender there.) But what a staggering shock it had been when, in those early dark days almost on the heels of Pearl Harbor, Singapore had fallen to the forces of Tokyo. It stunned us all. The British Empire was no longer invincible. Moreover only later were we to learn that Lt. Gen. Arthur Percival had surrendered his 130,000 Commonwealth troops to Lt. Gen. Tomoyuki Yamashita's force of only 30,000 men, who themselves were dangerously low on ammunition. "Fortress Singapore" was the greatest capitulation that we in the outer reaches of the British Empire had ever heard of.

And what followed for us, with the Japanese advancing as far south as the Solomon Islands, was shock turning into alarm. Nothing like that was initially portended to New Zealand by the Pearl Harbor attack. We were rudely awakened.

Dad was too old for full-time military duty, but he and I both ended up in the Home Guard and were prepared, in sincere if picturesque fashion, to defend Makara. But Makara I feared was in no better shape than Singapore to hurl back the hordes of bayonet-wielding "Japs".

I was already enrolled at St. Patrick's College, which was situated next to the Basin Reserve in Wellington on Cambridge Terrace. The "old Grey Mother" was indeed getting old. Again my sisters had prepared me for college, the equivalent of high school in the United States, with tales of scholastic terror. But I actually liked the institution. Our teachers wore flowing black soutanes, and were all bright and witty characters.

Still driving us youngsters to school from Makara Beach, Dad now had to contend with wartime petrol rationing of eighteen imperial gallons a month. (Gasoline cost three shillings an imperial gallon.) To conserve his ration and contribute to the war effort, Dad would switch off the car's engine and coast for miles. It was dangerous but he soon had coasting in the Chevy down to a fine art. He could switch off the engine coming down Makara Hill into the city, and make it past Wellington's Karori Park. One time he actually managed to get up enough speed coming down Makara Hill to glide up and over another hill beyond the Karori post office, which allowed him to coast right into town. A record of sorts. It was all a question of gravity and speed—maybe Dad's rugby background had something to do with his coasting prowess.

I knew my parents had sacrificed a lot to send all of us to Catholic schools—they were not free, unlike public schools. So I tried to apply myself to my formal education as much as possible. The old chemistry lab was fun, and I could draw on my experience helping make up prescriptions at the chemist shop (pharmacy) where I had worked. There were nonetheless quite a few diversions at St. Pat's. The Tuck shop, full of soft drinks, sweets and lollies and always crowded at playtime, was the center of my extracurricular activities. We had a couple of handball courts and handball became my favorite game.

A short time after I arrived, the school began building a new gym. I had begun to play water polo at Thorndon Baths, the Te Aro pool and also at Hataitai Beach, mainly because several of the school prefects were trying to date Stellamaris and Quita and invited me to join agua-matches. They were good water polo players.

Every Friday the scholastic performance roll listing everyone's grades, the good and the bad, for the week was posted outside the assembly hall. This was after the entire student body crowded into the hall to receive a lecture from the rector.

During my second year Father "Bas" Blake became rector. He was a highly capable and likable scholar who had been to Oxford and the University of Grenoble in France besides the University of New Zealand. St. Pat's was a demanding school, much more rigorous than Marist Brothers'. Even so, some students smoked cigarettes in the toilet which others including me found stupid and stinking.

I preferred the aroma of my father's pipe and cigars.

My favorite teacher was Father Jock Neville who, eclectically enough, taught French as well as boxing. Neville had been in the seminary at Green Meadows, near the town of Napier, on New Zealand's North Island, when an earthquake destroyed it in 1931. He told us the safest place to be in an earthquake was in a doorway. In 1942 an earthquake struck Wellington while he was in charge of our class at St. Pat's. He was very much in control. He ordered us to take shelter under our desks as the plaster on the ceiling began falling. Interestingly, who was standing in the safest place—in the doorway? Father Neville.

Father Johnny Goulter coached our rugby team to victory while Father Jack Mannix, our English teacher, knew the poets well. Father Knight, who was nicknamed Will Hay after a British movie comedian, was an exceedingly boring bookkeeping teacher.

At St. Pat's I played cricket in summer and made the top team. I didn't like cricket. It was too slow. The important games were always on Saturday. Still we did get to wear long white pants, which was a welcome change. No young lady, I learned, wanted to go out with a boy in shorts with bare and unbecoming hairy legs.

Then I boxed. With Uncle Brian as my coach I had boxing made. Makara proved an ideal training camp for the championship fight in the new St. Pat's gym, which had been inaugurated in 1941 by Prime Minister Peter Frazer. To reach my heavyweight title bout I beat a fast-moving contender, and then was matched for the championship against a big, lumbering opponent, Harry Cutler, who was as blind as a bat without his glasses.

On the day of my championship fight against Cutler, Mum made tripe for lunch. That evening my stomach was so queasy when I saw how crowded the gym was it was not the tripe but stage fright that made me think I couldn't come out of my corner. But I won on points and Uncle Brian immediately lectured me on how I could have done better. My father was proud and my mother thankful I had not been floored. I was glad to get it over and hated to think that the following year, 1943, I would have to defend my title. I was given the big silver trophy with a boxer on it and my name was added to the list of other St. Pat's heavyweight champions on the trophy. I was allowed to keep it for the year, and then had to return it in exchange for a little four-inch-high miniature.

I took St. Pat's compulsory Cadet Corps training seriously, spending hours shining the brass belt buckle and buttons of my uniform with Brasso. Our "lemon squeezers"—wide-brimmed felt hats—were finally changed for the small, rakish glengarry caps that could be opened up in cold weather to become balaclavas that covered most of the head. There was nothing one could do about the coarse khaki tunic and shorts. We were issued .303 rifles and bayonets.

Every Wednesday was parade day at St. Pat's and then annually there was Barracks Week at Prince of Wales Park. During my last year we had veterans from the bloody Greece and Crete campaign as training instructors. By then hundreds of graduates from St. Pat's had gone off to war. Many didn't return.

I wanted to be the sergeant major of cadets, which was the top position. You needed a strong voice to shout orders to the entire corps. I did get to lead a company and would yell, "Company will march in column of route, quick march!", and our drum-and-bugle band would strike up a march. Wellington College, on the other side of the Basin Reserve and our chief rival, had a bagpipe band. Being part Celt I loved the bagpipes and was sorry St. Patrick's hadn't endowed us with Irish pipes.

My shiny buttons paid off. I was among a group chosen to undergo special military training, with cadets from other schools around the North Island, at the military camp at Dannevirke. It was tough, regular-army training that included a mock battle. One of our instructors was Captain Hulme, who had won the Victoria Cross in North Africa and had returned to train military recruits.

There were few concessions to our status as students. One night I couldn't make it to the latrine, having developed diarrhea. It was a moonless night and I was caught by necessity on the parade ground. As I returned to my bunk I made out many other figures on the parade ground in the very same predicament. The next morning, before we could even report sick, the sergeant major marched us up and down the parade ground, which by then exuded the same odor as the latrine.

I was determined to get top marks at school in order to be chosen to apply for a scholarship to Sandhurst, Britain's leading military academy, or to its equivalent in the Southern Hemisphere, the Duntroon Royal Military College in Australia. My life began to revolve around Duntroon. A friend of my sisters, Ron Hassett, two classes ahead of me at St. Pat's, had won a scholarship to Duntroon. He was later to become commander of the New Zealand Army.

Wasn't I one of the sons of Rudyard Kipling who as a small boy wanted above all to join the Imperial Army, no less, and become an officer and gentleman in the Bengal Lancers and serve on India's North-West frontier fighting fierce Afghan tribes?

Furthermore my great-grandfather had been a professional soldier in the Imperial Army and come to New Zealand on the Queen's orders. Jock Warnock, my godfather, who had a hotel in Queenstown on beautiful Lake Wakatipu in the South Island, had entered the ranks of the famous Scottish Black Watch regiment at 16. He served with those Highlanders in the Great War, during which he had been wounded and taken prisoner by the Germans who forced him to work in the salt mines despite his wounds.

Then one day I received the Duntroon application papers. One of the requirements for New Zealanders turned out to be that both sets of your grandparents had to have been born either in New Zealand or in the British Isles. With a German-born grandfather, I was excluded. I felt terrible. It was a third sting of discrimination. Being part Irish in this very British society had been a step down the ladder, but being Irish-German, as well as Catholic in this predominantly Protestant country, really made me an underdog.

Whether it was the values my parents implanted, or growing up in Makara, or simply my own perception of things, I was solidly in the corner of the underdog. Meanwhile my disenchantment with the military was growing. At the rate the war in the Pacific was going I began to believe that the Japanese would eventually take New Zealand. We were eminently unprepared as far as I was concerned.

Several times a week, after getting home, Dad and I would change into our Home Guard uniforms. (Dad's friends at army headquarters had outfitted him with the latest uniform, which was referred to as the new battle dress and had a blouse-type tunic with no brass buttons. The rest of us had to make do with old World War I uniform with a panoply of brass buttons.) The training meetings and lectures were held at the Makara Hall. Its polished wood dance floor suffered from heavy army hobnailed boots worn by the farmers. (Our old Hall didn't survive the war; it had deteriorated to the point where it was finally pulled down and replaced by another, modern hall built along the main road.)

Dad and his dairy farmer friends John and Les Monk considered themselves scouts—Dad, because he was an expert hunter and crack shot, and the Monks because they knew the terrain so well from mustering cattle and sheep. The self-styled "Makara Scouts" sounded romantic, like the flamboyant Australian Light Horse Brigade galloping to glory. However, the Makara Home Guard was hardly dashing.

Makara Beach was transformed, but I was far from convinced it would be the Japanese's Gallipoli. Gun emplacements were dug on the beach above the high-water mark. Barbed wire was strung along the sand and big iron tank traps were put in place. Our beloved sand dunes were leveled to provide a clear field of fire. Real soldiers were on guard duty. Big, long-range, 8-inch guns were positioned on the hill overlooking Cook Straits.

Our garage served as headquarters for the New Zealand Army contingent stationed at Makara Beach, and a field telephone was installed which was quite an event. The nearest residential telephone had been at the Hawkins farm. It was a party line and it usually took a while to reach the other person whenever you had need of the phone. We rarely did. We thought of it as an instrument to be used only in an emergency, such as calling a doctor or an ambulance. But now that there was a war on we had to guard that rudimentary telephone system.

Uncle Brian, who was back in the Army, was assigned as a guard at the wireless relay station that had been built on a hill in rabbit country on the Giddings sheep station. There were guns protecting this communications outpost. However the only thing that came ashore at Makara Beach was oil in big 50-gallon drums. They had no markings and all we could surmise was that they had come from a torpedoed ship or German submarine.

One night my father and a couple of friends were going rabbit shooting up at Castlepoint, in the Wairarapa, and were halted in front of Gaskin's farm house, near the bridge where we had had our first accident as kids in the Nash. There were now Army road-blocks leading to Wellington. That night the password was "willow," but having had a couple of beers and feeling ridiculous Dad and his buddies said "Japanese consul." They were held before the chain across the road for twenty minutes as punishment for their unwelcome joke.

Makara was by now a different place in other respects. Electricity had finally reached us in 1939. Each night before the last pole was dug and the wire strung on it, we watched the progress as one farmhouse after another was lit up like a birthday cake. At the beginning there was no thought of conserving electric power and the farmer, once he got electricity, would switch on all the lights in his house and sometimes sleep with them on. However, the ensuing electric bill encouraged conservation.

As we passed the Hawkins' at any hour we could hear their new radio blasting away. Our house likewise changed with electricity. We would rush home to hear another radio episode of *Fu Manchu*. There was now the relayed BBC to listen to as well as the Australian radio import, *Dad and Dave of Snake Gully*, and the loquacious Kiwi lady commentator, "Aunt Daisy." Our new little white radio had an honored position in the kitchen. The next most treasured acquisition—especially by Mum—was an electric stove.

Yet no one could forget the war.

Jack Neilson, Scandy Neilson's eldest son, whom I admired and had helped with the digging of the last electric poles before our house, was one of Makara's first to leave for the war. He went as a sapper (one who lays, detects or disarms mines). An exploding mine eventually killed him.

Besides all my other chores and sports, during one vacation period I took lessons on the old Hotchkiss machine-gun at the Wellington Yacht Club. No sooner did I become proficient at dismantling and assembling this ancient weapon than it was made officially obsolete.

I had more luck in the Home Guard learning to use the Thompson submachine gun, which became a major weapon during the war. And when we went to Moa Point for hand grenade practice, one elderly Home Guardsman sent us all running when his hand froze over the grenade after he had pulled out the pin. Our instructor managed to unfold the elder's hand while keeping the leveler pressed down, and throw the grenade over the rocks to explode in the water.

One weekend we Home Guardsmen from Makara went on maneuvers. Dad knew better and had a cooked-up excuse to avoid the mission. The rest of us were assigned several hills, near the turnoff from Makara Road to Johnsonville. Our officer instructed us to take up defensive positions amongst pine trees, warning that at some time during the night regular troops would "attack" us. The officer then vanished (heading back to a comfortable bed in Wellington we suspected) leaving us to "defend" the hills of Makara as best we could. We had bombs—little paper bags filled with flour—which were to be used to mark the enemy in hand-to-hand combat! We also had a few blanks for our almost obsolete P. 14 rifles.

The farmer-Guardsmen, all bedded down in the pine needles, were soon fast asleep leaving me, the youngest, on sentry duty with instructions to wake them at the first sighting of the enemy.

There was just enough moon for me to make out strange shapes in the distance and suffering from what might be called the Singapore syndrome—fear of being caught from behind—I crawled along our perimeter and spent hours trying to distinguish between gorse bushes and "enemy troops." Suddenly I heard what I took to be a soldier creeping up the hill. My head kept low, my heart pounding, I hissed: "You blokes wake up! The enemy's down there!" I shook them awake and, as they protested, I hustled them into position. "It's a bloody possum you bloody bastard," yelled one irate farmer whose voice broke the sound barrier.

Well past midnight I roused them again. This time it was not even an animal. By now I was imagining things.

And there was generalized grumbling in the ranks about my performance as a trigger-happy sentry. I recalled the stories Uncle Brian had told of officers being shot by their men while trying to order them over the top in the trench warfare in France during the First World War. (Decades later, among American troops in Vietnam, it was called "fragging.") I remember thinking to myself; thank God these undisciplined farmers have no live ammo! They didn't have the good sense to relieve me during the night, so as dawn was breaking I awakened all the sleeping Guardsmen once more and told them we had to be prepared to repel a sunrise attack. I based my warning on the strategic fact that the Indians in Hollywood westerns always attacked at dawn. This time the grumbling reached near-mutiny proportions.

Our officer arrived later in the morning, clean-shaven and refreshed after a good night's sleep, to inform us that the regular troops would not be coming after all, that "there was a change of signals during the night." When I unwisely suggested that our troop needed a communications system, perhaps a field telephone, several of the farmers pelted me with dry chips of cow dung believing that such modern instruments would disturb their sleep even more than I had.

Another time we staged our own mock battle on home ground. We had helped construct a number of deep trenches at the base of the hills. Their field of fire was across a flat Hawkins cow pasture. Within this field of fire the "Japanese invaders" would be mowed down. The idea was to have all kinds of second and third lines of defense, if the enemy managed to get ashore.

In our daylight mock battle, I was one of the attacking Japanese. While our invading troops were about to maneuver for a frontal assault across the cow pasture, I asked permission from my superior to slip away with an extra load of flour bombs and execute a guerrilla attack from the rear. The Japanese had taught us in Singapore how effective this tactic could be.

Permission granted I ran around and climbed a hill out of sight of the defenders, and crept down the steep hill until I was in position directly above the trenches of the Makara Scouts. They were looking out for us to attack across the field as in more traditional warfare, not from behind their backs. I could hear them discussing the price of milk and wool. Standing, basically on top of them, I let go with a barrage of flour bombs. It was total destruction of this unit of the Makara Home Guard.

The farmers climbed out of the trenches covered in flour yelling, "You silly bugger!" I was all prepared to receive the Victoria Cross, the highest medal awarded by the British Army for valor. Instead one home-guardsman-farmer turned to my father and said, "Bernie can't you do something about this son of yours? Keep the young sod at home." There was a general murmur of agreement from the rest of the defeated troopers busy brushing off the telltale flour.

One night in 1942 Major Wheeler of the local Army Reserve

(I was keen on his daughter) came to Makara Hall to decide on who would be promoted to corporal and so command and drill the Makara Home Guard. Dad later recalled the incident, laughing, "You got very sour (upset) . . . I told the major, give it to my son, he is soldier-mad, he is being trained at college." Then, my father reminisced, Major Wheeler called him aside, out of earshot, and asked, "If the Japs land would you take orders from your son?" Dad continued: "It was during smoko and we were drinking tea and you were munching on those great biscuits and I told him, 'No, if the Japs land it's every man for himself.' The major said, 'In that case, you [meaning Dad] will have to be corporal.'"

Promoting Dad over me was too much. I was fifteen and decided Makara was now vulnerable and expendable. I was certain that Japanese troops could come ashore at Makara Beach and go rabbit-hunting without the slightest resistance from our Makara Scouts who would give away their own positions by their deafening snoring. I quit the Makara Home Guard and joined the Royal New Zealand Air Force cadets in Wellington for a brief period, believing we might have a better chance of beating the Japanese in the air.

In a way I was right. Years after the war it was disclosed that a Japanese warplane had flown over Makara and Wellington. It was the Germans, not the Japanese, who allegedly landed in New Zealand. However they didn't elect to come ashore at Makara Beach. Instead the Germans claimed that they went ashore from U-boat U862 near Napier, located several hundred miles north of Makara, and were not after rabbits, but fresh milk.

Under the command of Cmdr. Heinrich Timm, this German U-boat operating out of Singapore had sunk eight Allied freighters in the Indian Ocean and Tasman Sea in 1944 and 1945. Nonetheless the crew's most brazen action, it might be said, was against a New Zealand dairy herd—and illustrated how pathetically unprepared my country was to repel any kind of enemy horde.

The story, one of the most bizarre and amusing to come out of the war, was revealed nearly forty years later by the U-boat's commander. The submarine in question had been ordered to Napier to sink an Allied ship loading meat there for the war effort. The ship experienced engine trouble and remained in port. The submariners lurking offshore surfaced to watch the young ladies dancing on the town's seafront bandstand. The German sailors had an understandable craving for fresh milk and, under cover of darkness, a detachment from the submarine sneaked ashore undetected rounded up a dairy herd, and literally milked the cows on enemy terrain. When the news broke in 1995 of the milk raid by the Germans, Frank Steiner, whose dairy farm was closest to Napier, said he indeed recalled a day when his cows had turned up suspiciously dry. Much later it was also revealed that a Japanese reconnaissance plane did fly over Wellington.

We had lost contact with Father Des Scanlon by the time Japan entered the war. We later heard that the Japanese, in May 1942, had landed in the Solomons. It was as far south as they got.

War fever continued to grip Wellington. New Zealand was finally invaded—-by friendly Yanks. The streets, trains and trams were filled with U.S. Marines. The pubs did what they could to be as liberal as possible with their whiskey ration (Scotch was particularly precious). But they could do little about cooling the beer. Ironically New Zealand soldiers were already in their third year of fighting as part of the British 8th Army in North Africa against the German and Italians, while the U.S. forces (Marines) were in New Zealand training to stop the Japanese and their advance southward. The Japanese had routed the British in Burma, Hong Kong, Malaya and Singapore; the Dutch from their East Indies possessions; and were in the process of trying to take the huge island of New Guinea while the smaller islands of New Britain and Rabaul had fallen as had the Solomons. The Japanese Imperial Army was at our doorstep and they did eventually bomb Darwin, Australia's most northern town. And all we thought the Japanese could make was cheap and worthless toys.

The U.S. Marines were bivouacked at a Camp on a hill facing the sea above Mackay's crossing close to Paekakariki about 20 miles north of the city and they were made welcome. Some even ventured to Makara. Both Quita and Stellamaris worked at an USO, the United Service Organization post that provided hospitality for servicemen and women. The local USO was on Manners Street in Wellington. I forget now the names of the Marines of the First Marine Division whom we welcomed to Makara. One was a fine piano player and gave us some terrific jazz concerts.

In July, a particularly cold and rainy month in Wellington, we had watched, as the wharves became crowded with ships and war materiel. U.S. Marines who had been training in Paekakariki were saying goodbye. Then in early August we heard the news that those same men of the 1st Marine Division, under the command of Maj.Gen.Alexander A. Vandergrift USMC, had landed in the Solomon Islands, taken Tulagi, and were fighting on Guadalcanal 20 miles across the channel.

* * *

One day in mid-October 1942 I was called out of class at St. Pat's. I had an important visitor. At first I didn't recognize Father Des Scanlon. I thought he was a U.S. Marine or U.S. Navy officer, as he was dressed in a light tropical khaki uniform of the US services. We embraced and sat down near the handball courts, and he told the incredible story of his escape from Guadalcanal. He had just arrived by boat from the Solomons. I'll never forget the awe with which he talked of the air war. Des spared me the details of all the blood and gore of America's first offensive of the War. For him and the others at the Catholic mission, it was an incongruous sight on an island so close to the Stone Age—witnessing man's modern fighting machines streaking over the clerics to deliver bombs on the enemy. The mission was close enough to the action to feel the "earth shake beneath our feet" from the shock of the bombs.

Watching this extraordinary air war was nearly their undoing, Father Des explained. While they waved the American planes on, one peeled off and machine-gunned the mission and another dropped a bomb. Bullets pierced the schools and refectory but no one was wounded. (The American pilots who dropped a bomb on the mission and machine-gunned it, later stated that they had been told no Europeans were on that part of the island and, that they had taken gunfire from the Japanese post near the mission.)

It served as a timely warning and ended their sky show as Mission head, Bishop Henri Aubin, decided they should move away from the mission compound, which was obviously a target, to the safety of the dense jungle. Under the nose of the Japanese Post, they managed to move supplies to a hideout in the hills and quietly slip away from the mission.

Des' account of their escape from the Japanese was matter-of-fact. He reserved his praise for the loyal Solomon Islanders. Much later, reading an edition of *Marist Messenger* that carried an account of their escape, I realized Des had in no way romanced his story.

The war had come to the Solomons with the dawning of 1942. It began with Japanese dropping bombs on Tulagi with very little accuracy. By mid-January most of the civil government had been evacuated. There was no question of the missionaries leaving their flock. They were cut off from the world. On May 2 the Japanese landed unopposed on Tulagi, the British administrative capital of the Solomons. Then at the end of May they landed on Guadalcanal and set to work building an airfield at Lunga, some twenty miles from the mission headquarters at Visula. This airfield was to be vital to the Japanese push south to Australia and New Zealand.

Des said they had some early Japanese visits to the mission at Visale Bay, and one group commandeered a pig and had the missionaries cook it. Fearing the worst the missionaries tried their best to continue their work as usual. It was not until July 2 that T. Iosomoto, commander-in-chief of the Japanese forces on Guadalcanal, paid the mission a visit. He spoke some English and warned the missionaries that the islands were now Japanese territories and under martial law.

While his men made a complete inventory of the mission, a nine-man post, with a watchtower, was set up nearby.

Iosomoto told the missionaries he had orders to take all members of the mission back to Lunga, but he had decided one priest would be sufficient. They were surprised when the Japanese commander returned the priest a week later. The missionaries were repeatedly asked whether there were other Europeans on Guadalcanal. They consistently lied to their interrogators.

The other European were Australian and British Coastwatchers, members of a unique Royal Australian Navy intelligence network. These men were to play a vital role in the war in the Pacific islands. They were mostly volunteers who knew the islands and surrounding waters well as most of them were traders and planters. Equipped with radio transmitters they literally watched the coasts and alerted headquarters to enemy movements on sea, land and in the air. The information coastwatchers passed on from behind the enemy lines was vital to the war effort. There were even a few missionaries who became coastwatchers which actually put all missionaries in danger.

The Japanese requisitioned mission furniture and took away by force over a hundred islanders to labor on the airfield. In return the islanders were to receive Japanese citizenship.

On August 1, the coastwatchers on Guadalcanal smuggled word to the 500 Islanders pressed into working on the airfield that they should quietly disappear. They managed to do so. On August 3, American bombs rained down on the Japanese positions night and day. There was not one islander left on the airfield.

Finally, under cover of a heavy mist, the Americans approached the Solomons and four days later, August 7, 1942, seized the island of Tulagi and made their beachhead on Guadalcanal. The Japanese were taken by surprise. The nearly completed Lunga airfield was soon in Marine hands and they discovered the Japanese had left behind all the necessary heavy equipment to complete the airfield. They even left behind an ice-making machine which the Marine's appreciated. But it was not long before the Japanese high command reacted and began pouring in reinforcement to engage in the bloody battle for Guadalcanal. The Japanese effort to slip troops onto the island was christened by the Marines the nightly "Tokio Express."

Meanwhile well hidden in the hills above their Visale mission were Bishop Aubin, Fathers Drugmans, McMahon, and Des Scanlon along with Sisters Evangeline, Theresa and George. They also had with them eight Solomon Island nuns.

On August 29, a Japanese Zero fighter plane crashed near their jungle hideout. The pilot had been badly shot up by the Americans. Out of compassion, the Sisters rendered him first aid. When he was assured that the nuns were not Americans in disguise, he put aside his pistol and thanked them in English. Two days later the Japanese raided the mission.

The bishop who had returned to the mission for medicine with a bad case of dysentery was tipped off by Islanders and managed to escape. From the hills, Des explained, "we saw another search party led by the Japanese pilot. So much for human kindness and compassion." But neither patrol found their hiding place thanks to a heroic youth from the mission. The Japanese were forcing him to guide them to the missionaries. He led them on a false trail and then tried to run away. The Japanese shot him dead. "If it hadn't been for this boy's heroic deed, we missionaries would have been taken prisoner and put to death like others," Des explained.

After they found the body of the youth and buried him it was decided to abandon the area and make a 50- miles trek across Guadalcanal to the other Catholic mission at Tangarare. This was no pleasurable hike. Not only did they have to keep alert for Japanese patrols in the midst of war but the jungle which covered the hills and rivers was also the enemy. It was malarial jungle with a lot of other tropical diseases. Even a small abrasion in the tropical jungle quickly turned into a lifethreatening sore. On the positive side, the missionaries counted on the aid of the loyal Solomon Islanders.

They finally made it to the Tangarare Mission Station without losing a single member of the group. There they met up with other members of their mission as well as a downed American pilot. The pilot had spent eight days paddling around in an inflatable rubber raft after being shot down.

In charge was an Australian naval officer who was on assignment on Guadalcanal as a coastwatcher. In total they numbered 17 Europeans at the Tangarare Mission as well as the wounded American pilot. Encircled by the Japanese who were moving closer every day, the group finally put an escape plan into action. The

15-ton ketch, *Bamada,* belonging to the Solomon Island (British) Protectorate Government, with a young Australian officer in charge, arrived. All departed on the ketch except Father E. De Klerk who decided he might still be able to serve his island flock.

The vessel hardly seemed to move but it chugged around the Japanese-held coast at six knots, and when it looked as if Japanese ships and barges in the process of landing more troops would overwhelm them, they radioed for an aerial escort. Even when they arrived off Lunga they were not safe. An American naval gunnery officer thought the ketch might be a Japanese submarine in disguise but wisely contacted officials on shore and learned the vessel's true identity before opening fire.

Des and fellow passengers were transferred to a small ship heading for French New Caledonia with two destroyers as escorts. Bishop Aubin chose to remain behind with the Solomon nuns. In Noumea the others changed ships and proceeded to Wellington.

They had escaped death. But not all the Marist missionaries were as lucky. Two priests and two nuns at Ruavatu, another Catholic mission station on Guadalcanal were held prisoner in a small shack, for a week by the Japanese and given hardly any food. When the U.S. Marines landed, the prisoners-Father Arthur Duhamel of Laurence, Massachusetts; Father Henri Oude Engberlink of Holland and French Sisters Marie-Odilia and Marie-Sylvia—were bayoneted in the neck and left to bleed to death.

Des said he had witnessed, from the hills, the night naval battle off Savo Island at the Western approach to Guadalcanal in what was later to be called Iron bottom Sound. The missionaries watched the flash of the guns in a battle that Des thought had lasted an hour. It ended in a victory for the Japanese Navy. More than a thousand Australian and American lives were lost in Iron bottom Sound that terrible night.

The Marines hung in there and completed the airfield which they named Henderson Field after a Marine dive bomber pilot killed in the battle of Midway.

It was only years later, after the war, that I learned from an article that appeared in *The New York Times* that Father Scanlon had become the priest on Norfolk Island, in the South Pacific, north of Australia, a much safer place than the Solomons had been. He passed away in 1987 at age 77. He had returned to the missions in the Solomons after the war but illness drove him off the islands. He had served a total of 12 years in very primitive conditions in the Solomons.

There was a footnote to his dramatic spiritual stewardship. As Pastor of Norfolk Island, he was known for his "canine altar servers." He had two well-behaved dogs that processed with the celebrant to and from the altar, and sat quietly and sedately at either side during services.

And this final personal footnote of the Pacific war: When the first wounded Marines arrived from Tulagi and Guadalcanal, I had accompanied my sisters to the Silverstream hospital where they we helping out as nurses' aides. There was one U.S. Marine who had taken a bullet in his spine and would never walk again. This wounded Marine had once been a boxer. As I was boxing at college at the time, I felt really bad for him, and helped comfort him by giving him massages.

CHAPTER 24

Sailing Before the Mast

The instant I saw her, it was love at first sight. She was beautiful. It happened during a lunch hour while I was strolling along the Wellington Wharf. Proud and tall she rode beside the wharf, a four-masted barque, a majestic square-rigger from another era.

The *Pamir* evoked a much stronger emotion than all my other loves, even the pretty "Land Girl" who had so recently arrived in Makara to do her bit of farming for the war effort and with whom I had finally got to dance. Or the lovely lass at the Courtenay Place milkshake bar who ditched me when she saw my hairy legs in St. Pat's short pants.

Though still a mere schoolboy, I couldn't take my eyes off the barque flying the New Zealand ensign, and I spent as much time as I could admiring her tall masts and 34 furled sails. And she was there every night in my dreams. I had a bad case of sea fever. As I grew into adolescence, the simple pleasures of rigorous farm work, fishing and all that an abundant nature had to offer had begun to wear off just a little. So was the embrace of Victorian morality.

My love affair with the *Pamir* would have been brief indeed had it not been for an incident which occurred that Easter in 1942. I was walking past the post office in Wellington when I found a package on the sidewalk. In the packet was a wad of paper money. Without a moment's hesitation I went looking for the owner. I reasoned that whoever had lost the cash must have been to the post office or one of the banks nearby. In the post office I asked an official whether someone had reported losing any money. When he said no I told him that I had found some money, that it should be counted and placed in a safe until the owner claimed it. The postal official and I counted it together. It was more than two hundred pounds and I left with a slip of paper as a receipt.

It was several weeks later that I received a call to go to the office of a famous barrister, Mr. Mazengarb. Mr. Mazengarb informed me that the money was his and that his secretary had dropped it *en route* to the bank. He gave me a five-pound reward, expressed his thanks and said that if there was ever anything he could do for me I should let him know. A month later, when I inquired about joining the crew of the *Pamir*, a New Zealand prize of war, I was told, "don't even try," scores or even hundreds of youths, all well connected, had tried and couldn't make it. "You'll need pull," I was told, "to join her crew." My family was no help. In fact they were very upset and steadfastly opposed to my going to sea in the *Pamir*. "No! And don't mention it again," both my Mum and Dad said, united in their opposition. They were unyielding. I was also unyielding. I was determined. The *Pamir* had sailed into Wellington in 1941 flying the Finnish flag. Technically Finland was on the wrong side in World War II and the New Zealand government, following Allied policy, seized the barque. And so for many young New Zealanders began a romantic wartime dream.

Seeking to learn more about the operation of a sailing ship, I searched Smith's secondhand bookstore. Though I devoured Dana's *Two Years Before the Mast*, I was less interested then in romantic books about sail and the sea but practical facts such a large sailing vessel. I needed to know about her stays and spars, masts and maze of rigging.

Both of my sisters opposed my going to sea. Whenever we saw a tipsy sailor about, they would sing,

"What can we do with a drunken sailor . . ."

It was difficult to defend my choice of a maritime service. We had no immediate relatives who had been sailors—only one distant cousin who had gone off on a whaling ship, without telling his wife. He just instructed her to keep his dinner warm. Two years later she nearly threw dinner at him when he returned.

Glenn Miller's smooth big-band music was the rage. *In The Mood* came to New Zealand. But I still had sailing on my mind. At last I would make my peace with the sea, or so I thought. The family remained adamantly opposed. Then I remembered Barrister Mazengarb's promise of help and went to see him. He said he would be glad to help me. He did. He arranged a meeting for me with the man who made the decisions about maritime matters. I was summoned to the presence of Mr. Finton Patrick Walsh, the powerful head of the seamen's union. He looked me over. "You are another of those who want to go on the *Pamir*, are you?" "Yes sir."

He said he knew my Uncle Frank (Diederich), who was also opposed to my joining the *Pamir*, believing I should follow the footsteps of Uncle Roy and become a lawyer. Mr. Walsh told me that I would be hired on the *Pamir's* next trip.

The barque was away on her second voyage to San Francisco under the New Zealand flag. There was no date for her return. I would have to wait. I waited, hoping.

When the *Pamir* did return and the hiring of the crew took place, I would have to show up at the seamen's hiring hall—opposite the wartime Army headquarters. It was the old system of hiring on a crew, as ancient as the maritime service. You stood there and waited. Waited to have a finger pointed at you or your name called. I didn't believe my name would ever be called. It was to be a long and anxious wait.

Meanwhile I had told my parents I was determined to go. My father was angry, my mother was still upset. Before I left St. Pat's, Father Blake, the rector, told me my marks were good and if I continued in school I could be a lawyer or anything else I might want to be. My Uncle Frank tried a generous bribe. He would give me a car and help me with my education tuition if I remained at school. I couldn't hear them; the sound of the sea drowned them all out.

Leaving St. Pat's, awaiting the return of the *Pamir*, I got a job at an old firm of freight-forwarding agents, McGowan and McGee, located on the quay almost next door to the Union Steamship Company. It gave me a chance to keep in touch with the approximate whereabouts of the *Pamir*, since the Union Steamship Company had been put in charge of the vessel after the New Zealand government seized it. McGowan and McGee had an office that was right out of Dickens, with high chairs and high desks. I enjoyed the work of checking bills of lading and other tasks connected with freight and the sea. I read Joseph Conrad and felt right at home.

When the day I had been waiting for finally arrived and the *Pamir* returned once more to King's Wharf, I was there to greet her. Then in the summer of 1943, the crucial moment arrived. We aspiring crewmen stood together, a nervous lot, in the crowded hiring hall. I was sure I would be passed over. But my name was called—and I wanted to shout for joy. Instead I quietly signed on as a sixteen-year-old cabin boy—one of twelve cabin boys in a total crew of 40—to sail on Voyage Three of the four-masted barque *Pamir* under the New Zealand flag.

It was a predictable farewell. I packed my new seabag and walked the Makara road for the last time all the way to the city. My father did not drive me. He had warned, "You have chosen to make your own bed, now you must lie in it." I went off to sea and the war, as the proverbial youth in search of adventure.

The salary was eight New Zealand pounds and two shillings and six pence a month. But I was not interested in the pay. I was in love, and the love of a windjammer, as beautiful and graceful as the *Pamir*, promised such an enriching experience that I would have willingly served aboard her without pay.

I had hardly I stepped onto her wooden deck, which I would soon be holystoning, when the bosun, Andy Keyworth, ordered me aloft to the fore royal. I looked up at the little spar brushing the clouds nearly 200 feet above the deck. (Actually the masts were 196 feet from keel to truck.) "Get up," the bosun commanded just as I was going to suggest that I get used to the rigging in short stages.

Once I reached the royal yardarm I discovered that my size-13 shoes were too large to fit into the last rattlings on the mast and I had to pull myself up by my arms. I was so high that I could look down at Wellington and even see Stellamaris' office window in the nearby railway station where she was an apprentice architect. It was a long way to the deck below. I would eventually learn to slide, hand over hand, down the stays at sea, which was a lot faster than climbing down the rigging.

Even when I was ordered down into the locker to slowly stow the huge anchor chain as we weighed anchor on that trip to San Francisco, I accepted what was the dirtiest and most monotonous job aboard ship goodheartedly.

When we finally reached the open sea after waiting days for a favorable northwesterly wind, and cleared Cook Strait, my last glimpse of land for 80 days was of Makara far astern.

That first day we made 293 nautical miles under all sails—except the gaff topsail—with our speed averaging 12½ knots. Our captain, David McLeish, was no timid soul and he liked to go all out on sail; one day we increased our speed to 15 knots—but not for long as the wind began blowing a gale. For two days it blew and for two days we were on deck—-actually in the rigging—taking in sail. What little sleep we caught was on the benches and tables in the mess in our soaking clothing.

I also had to triumph over seasickness. Yet even after I got my sea legs, the food was so awful (we had no refrigeration on that trip) it sometimes made you nauseous. But being out on a yard-arm, taking in sail in a gale, lashed by wind and rain, and riding with the ship's movements, was an exhilarating test. The footrope would swing dangerously high behind as you leaned over the yard-arm to grapple with the canvas, which was as stiff as a board. All that was left to cling to the yardarm with, were your stomach muscles.

For me the *Pamir* was the ultimate challenge. In a sense I had come full circle from early childhood. My old companions from Makara Beach, the wind and the sea were once again in charge. It was to them that I now had to pray. Stricken by homesickness as we battered gale winds, I heard my father's voice again and again, "You made your bed, lie in it . . ." I had no bed but a bunk and, braced in my bunk in heavy seas, wet and stinking (nor of course did we have showers), I silently cried for Makara and my family. Still, I possessed an abundance of healthy and happy Makara memories.

As the Maori warriors before, I liked to think that I too was sailing away in search of something more exciting and promising. It was wartime, so there were the ritual added precautions and restrictions, such as complete blackout at sea and radio silence, as well as constant lookout for enemy submarines.

There were rough times. And good times. There was always excitement. And there were moments of sheer ecstasy. Under a full moon that accentuated the whiteness of her sails (36,853 square feet of canvas) filled by a steady trade wind, the *Pamir* sliced with ease through the phosphorescent sea as flying fish darted over the waves. Suddenly there was another sound besides the creaking of the rigging; was it Bach or Beethoven? From the officers' deck came the strains of a violin concerto. Ake Liewendahl, the Finnish third mate, who had remained with the ship when the rest of the Finnish crew went ashore to wait out the war in Wellington, was playing for his personal enjoyment—and perhaps that of the entire crew. The combination of sound and setting was overpowering. The magic of this windjammer, sails billowing in the trade winds, still evokes that thrill more than 50 years later.

She returned our love by carrying us safely across the Pacific. She spoke to us through the big wooden steering wheel, as big as a man and with the kick of a mule when the air was light and we lost steerage. We hated the doldrums. Nor did we wish the *Pamir* had engine power to move us out of the windless becalmed state. Engines would have ruined this beautiful ship. That first trip took 80 days, fifteen hours, and fifteen minutes sailing time between Wellington, New Zealand, and San Francisco, California, and we had sailed 10,243 nautical miles, nearly twice the actual distance between the two ports. Because we were at the mercy of the winds our average speed had been 5.5 knots. Dropping anchor off Treasure Island in San Francisco Bay, the *Pamir* startled a lot of local sea dogs and even American airmen. We found it humorous that pilots from Alameda Naval Air Station would later visit us, and come aboard ship to marvel at the barque. As we caught the westerlies off Frisco, blimps on submarine patrol flew overhead perhaps believing that at last they had sighted the legendary *Flying Dutchman.*

On our return voyage to Wellington I found that my old demon friend from Makara had not forgotten me. He was lying in wait to surprise me and the rest of the crew. We were only a few miles from our homeland, the wind had subsided. It was during the evening dogwatch and we could see lights ashore. I would be able to see Makara in the morning. There was a great deal of excitement aboard, as we prepared to enter port. That trip had covered a distance of 6,517 nautical miles and had taken 58 days and five hours.

Bosun Andy Keyworth described well what happened next in Jack Churchouse's book, *The Pamir Under the New Zealand Ensign:*

> "Shortly after 6 o'clock the sea rippled and the lifeless sails filled once again. But suddenly all hell let loose. Within minutes the wind was blowing at least force eight and much stronger than that before the night was out. The *Pamir* staggered, struck by a thousand furies, reeled and turned to run before the gale.
>
> "All hands appeared on deck, none needed calling, and began the night-long struggle to steady the barque and bring her under control. So began the fight to save the sails. Long backbreaking hours stretched out on the yards clawing at the canvas, dragging it in inch by inch. Tucking each fold under bellies to hold it while hands reached out anew to grasp more of the bucking, slashing, searing cloth. The heartbreak on a lower topgallant when, with the sail finally gathered in ready to pass the gasket, a fraction of a second's inattention and 'bang'—away it went again from those on the yard and worse, took a buntline with it. So they began again. It was even harder this time than before. Goodness knows how but they got it in. How long? Two hours on that yard and what was remembered most was the cold. How

they stood the cold will never be known. Nine sails were lost
that awful night although many more than that were saved
by the efforts of all on board."

The gale caught me on the bowsprit taking in the flying jib
(more sailors have been lost off the bowsprit than from aloft) and
in that angry, churning sea and howling wind I knew it was the
devils of Makara at it again, welcoming me home and showing me
that they were still masters of my fate. Managing to scramble back
aboard I went aloft to join the fight to save the sails. We 12 neo-
phyte crewmen (cabin boys) now had salt water in our veins and
welcomed the challenge even though it was a really tough fight.

Trip Four took 79 days, 20 hours and 37 minutes from
Wellington to San Francisco covering 10,519 nautical miles at an
average speed of 5.5. knots, and the return trip, 51 days, 18 hours
and nine minutes, came close to the record between the two cities.
It was my last voyage aboard the *Pamir*. She had provided me with
enough adventure to fill a lifetime and I was terribly sad to leave
her, but I knew we had to part. My love for that elegant sailing
vessel will endure until the grave.

It was during that last voyage that my conscience had begun
to bother me. I felt I was shirking my war duty by carrying non-
essential freight back and forth between San Francisco and
Wellington. So I volunteered to fill a vacancy aboard an U.S. Merchant Marine ship. There was no problem in the fact that I was a
New Zealander. Many non-United States citizens served in the
U.S. Merchant Marine during the war.

The U.S. ship which I joined was the *Camas Meadows*, a T-2
class oil tanker, of the type that helped fuel the Allies' Pacific war
machine against Japan. Like the World War II Liberty and Victory
ships, the T-2 tankers were essential to winning that epic struggle,
and we who sailed on them took pride in that fact. I was to serve
aboard two of these armed but highly vulnerable oil tankers during the conflict.

With deadweight of 16,600 tons and a speed of nearly 15
knots, the T-2 tankers could carry more than 140,000 barrels of

high-octane aviation gasoline and/or other, heavier fuels. A total of 532 of these tankers were built during the war. They were the forerunners of the giant supertankers constructed after the war.

When I left New Zealand on my first tanker both my sisters, Quita and Stellamaris came to see me off. I shall never forget my embarrassment when Quita lovingly ran down the quay shouting somewhat hysterically that I shouldn't go, that I was "going to be killed," that the petroleum tanker was a floating coffin in wartime! And indeed these tankers were referred to as "Kaiser's coffins," after their famous wartime American ship builder, Henry Kaiser. Some were rumored to break up in a storm but the two vessels I served on were fine ships, and after the rustic experience of living aboard the *Pamir*, the tankers were more like palaces than a coffin. It was like stepping from one century into another.

Imagine white, laundered sheets in place of heavy wool blankets, (We had to wash occasionally in salt water), a variety of tasty, healthful meals and ice cream instead of the unappetizing *Pamir* fare of canned bully beef and tapioca dessert. The *Pamir* cook had little to work with but at least he frequently provided some unintentional vitamins. Though no fault of his own he baked from flour bread that more often than not was heavily laden with weevils. We called it our daily vitamin ration and the only fresh food.

Our water ration aboard the *Pamir* divided among our crew of 40, were a gallon and a half per person per day. A gallon of that was allotted to the galley for cooking. The brackish half-gallon left over for drinking was no treat. By comparison, on the T-2 tanker there was plenty of drinking water and the coffeepot was always perking.

The refrigerator plant on the *Pamir*, powered by a "donkey engine" was extremely temperamental. Despite the heroic efforts of the motorman who operated the little engine, located under the poop deck, (it once kicked like a mule and broke the motorman's arm) failed it all too often to freeze our perishable foodstuffs. For example on my first trip the perishable foodstuffs soon perished. Rose's lime juice probably saved us from scurvy. (Each of the twelve cabin boys had their assigned day to scrub both quarters of the

cabin port and starboard watches and mess. The bleaching prop-
erties of lime juice, we discovered, were a great help in giving a
clean, white look to the wooden deck.)

The crew was divided into two watches on the *Pamir*. They
were port and starboard watches. In the evening, each watch worked
a four-hour turn at steering, lookout, trimming the sails and necessary deck work. Depending on the weather it was possible to
catnap when not otherwise occupied. Early evening was broken
down by the dogwatches which were between 4 to 6 p.m. and 6 to
8 p.m. During the day both watches worked. It meant that we
seldom managed to sleep longer than four hours in the evening.

On the tankers there was no shortage of sleep. On the *Pamir*
we sailed under complete radio silence and even when one of our
crew came down with a serious case of appendicitis the crew voted
to break radio silence and call for assistance to save his life. The
tough Kiwi captain refused. Miraculously the patient survived the
trip to be treated in San Francisco. On the tanker we had a crew of
50 men, and we received our mail in the islands where we stopped.

Air-conditioning hadn't arrived aboard ships but on the tankers we had a fresh air system that made my cabin—my own cabin!—
a relaxing reading room. On the islands it was possible to exchange
books with the crews of other ships and while much of the literature was trashy sex—sailors delight—there were also some excellent authors. On the barque there had been little time for reading.
On the tankers it became my passion.

The *Pamir*, painted black and white—not wartime grey—had
no armament. Its two obsolete rifles were used to shoot sharks.
The tankers were armed. On the stern we carried anti-submarine
depth charges. There was a three-inch gun on the bow and another on the stern. Anti-aircraft guns were also positioned aft and
amidships. The U.S. Navy gunner crew attached to the tankers
were members of the U.S. Navy Armed Guard. At sea they also
trained us in the use of the guns.

The two tankers I served on sailed alone the wide, expansive
Pacific Ocean unhindered by convoys. When given a submarine
alert, and this usually happened in the Atlantic Ocean which we

also sailed without convoys, we ran a zigzag course. *En route* from Curacao to New York—where I passed Coast Guard tests and volunteered for service on a new tanker, the *Port Republic*—we changed course so often that any submarine commander would have become dizzy at his periscope.

In New York, I choose to return to the Pacific Theater of war on the *Port Republic* where sailing to the Persian Gulf oil refineries, our major concern was avoiding Arab dhows and Indian fishing boats on moonless nights. My tanker crossed the Torres Straits between Australia and New Guinea. Approaching the Pacific islands in the war zone we were aware that the enemy was in the sky. We often itched to try out our guns on a Japanese kamikaze but our only shooting was target practice.

Under sail on the *Pamir* we became as one with the wind and the ocean. At night, the creaking of the large, beautiful vessel was like a lullaby. By contrast on the modern tankers there was little such attachment or contact. In fact it was an almost impersonal relationship between ship crew and the ocean. Unlike the *Pamir* on which we caught Bonita, on the tanker we saw only flying fish that flew onto our long, low decks.

In spite of the tankers' modern conveniences and relatively easy living—even though the fuel-laden ship promised to become a fireball if torpedoed or bombed —I pined for the *Pamir* and my dreams were of that fabulous barque. The nostalgia wouldn't go away.

The end of the war caught us in the Indian Ocean heading for the Pacific with a cargo of fuel oil. We were ordered to change course for Singapore where Britain's Lord Louis Mountbattan commander of Southeast Asian Allied forces, took the surrender of the Japanese occupying forces.

It was in Singapore that I received a telegram from home. It read: "Stellamaris entered the convent Easter Sunday all pleased and happy. Signed: Mother." It was a shock but she had often said she might enter the convent. I had lost my jitterbug partner. She was a great dancer.

It was not until June 1946 that I left the *Port Republic*, receiv-

ing my discharge from the U.S. Coast Guard in Houston, Texas. I
returned to Makara, proving my dear sister Quita wrong. I managed to return in time to attend the church ceremony of the new
Sister Benignus—Stellamaris—becoming a Sister of Mercy. The
ceremony was heart rendering even though I had never seen her so
happy.

EPILOGUE

They Are Gone Now

They are gone now, those scenes of long ago. Nature has almost totally reclaimed the enchanting never-never land of our childhood. It was as if that life existed only in our consciousness, its secrets well sealed from outsiders. Seagulls still ride the wind and screech at the sea but the roaring surf and howling wind are no longer intimidating.

Our house is still there with its white picket fence. I don't know who lives there. Our father sold it years ago after we children, by then grown, had gone our individual ways. Yet as the wind eases and the sun slides into the sea, nostalgia rises and a flurry of heart-rending memories of our vanished lives makes one shiver. The *Pamir* is also gone. In 1957, thirteen years after I left her, the *Pamir*, ironically by then sailing under the West German flag, went down in a hurricane south of the Azores with only six survivors and 80 crew lost.

I look back, not with any resentment at the distant geographic location of my childhood, but with deep feeling and to thank God that I was lucky enough to grow up in a place where the impersonal forces of nature were so very personal and spiritual. We were colonials from the antipodes and at Makara Beach we were even more remote and withdrawn from the world.

My father, self-effacing Kiwi that he was, might well have dismissed the reflections on these pages as "all bloody rot," and cautioned me not to be "a bloody skite." Before he died in 1992 at age 93, he and I had gone back together to Makara. Then residing in Martinborough he hadn't wanted to go. As usual he drove the car.

That afternoon, in 1985, he was pensive and said very little. The visit was obviously a painful one for him. He hadn't visited the old homestead in years. Now it clearly stirred too many memories. We all had strong, conflicting emotions about Makara.

My mother had died on July 19th, 1981, on her father's birthday, and the day after mine. Death for Mum came at 86 years of age, many miles away from Makara, in the picturesque pastureland of the Wairarapa Valley. With its vineyards and deer farms and sheep stations it was in deep contrast to Makara. Mum and Dad are buried in the Wairarapa Valley surrounded by New Zealand's picture-postcard scenery and now famous Pinot Noir grapes. Not far from where great-grandfather Diederich first settled when he brought his family out from Germany at the beginning of 1876. It was only fitting that my brothers and then finally Mum and Dad should have moved back to the bountiful valley after nearly 40 years at Makara.

"It was great growing up here," I told Dad and a million memories of Makara flooded back. "Thanks." "Oh, don't be silly," he answered gruffly trying to hide his own emotions. "It wasn't. It was hard on your mother." We were returning to the clement weather of the Wairarapa Valley.

How the wind of Makara cries out now in its solitude. The fishermen's huts are gone and there was talk of making our old seaside playground into a national reserve, a preserve of nature in the raw. Few of the farms we knew are left. It was a rare case in which the natural environment defaced by settlers had at last won a reprieve. Its vulnerability to the elements had made it a habitat only for sea birds and other fauna. Some native birds like the *pukeko* have returned and one was nesting where the Hawkins' cowshed once stood; even the *morepork* has been heard at night.

At the little dairy shop facing the beach next to where the Bailey family lived, Dad and I stopped for a soft drink. I asked the shopkeeper whether he had ever heard of the Diederich family, who had lived around the corner in the house with the tennis court. He shook his head, no. I was overcome with sadness. The nostalgia was overpowering. A family life gone by and forgotten.

Mum had done so much for the valley and so had Dad. Testimony to our fleeting intrusion was the still visible scar behind our house where Dad had scooped out the hill in order to build the tennis court.

I felt like putting a little plaque up on the side of the road before our house with the inscription: "Diederich family: 1928-1970." But the ghosts of Makara are best left alone.

As we drove back to Wellington, ending our visit, Dad. said with certain finality, "I'll not go back there again."

Among the dozen or so guidebooks on New Zealand encountered at a Borders book store in Miami, Florida, was a 1993 edition of the *New Zealand Handbook*, by Jane King, which listed Makara in the index.

It was no surprise to read under the heading, "Wellington Walks," about one of the area's hiking routes: "The six-km Makara track, part of the New Zealand Walkways network, starts and finishes at Makara Beach (16 km northwest of Wellington). This popular walk lets hikers experience some remote and rugged coastal scenery, fabulous views, hilly farmland, and good swimming at sheltered beaches. The 'Track' requires good fitness and takes about four hours RT: note that the inner section is closed during August and September for lambing. Wear good boots, and take warm clothing (you'll be exposed to the wind, and quite possibly blown along the track in places!), and water—nothing drinkable along the route.

It's also another good place to take a picnic. To get there from Wellington you need your own transportation and a detailed map (the Information Centre provides a free brochure): head for Karori Rd. in the western suburb of Karori West. Take Makara Rd. west and continue to Makara Beach where the walkway is clearly signposted."

I felt like adding, "You won't walk alone. The ghosts of Makara will accompany you."

Still perched on the hill above our house, where Moldy and Zelda Monk used to live, is now an enchanting home of the New Zealand writer Yvonne Du Fresne, whose Danish ancestors, by

coincidence, came to New Zealand on the same ship as the
Diederich family.

POSTSCRIPT

Our brother Brian as a member of the New Zealand army saw Post-World War II service in occupied Japan. He rarely discussed the reactions he felt after visiting the destruction wrought by the atom bombs. In civilian life he traveled extensively for business and pleasure and eventually, never losing his wonderful sense of humor, returned to the Wairarapa Valley to farm with brother Patrick.

Brother Geoffrey's love of horses was a lifelong one. Throughout the years he has raised and trained racehorses, jumpers and polo ponies. However, even though he was the great dreamer in the family he could never bring many of those dreams to fruition. Two of Geoffrey's and his wife Diana's sons found the climate of Australia's Northern Territory to their liking and settled down there. Two others sons remained in the Wairarapa Valley, farming. Rebecca, Geoffrey's and Diana's only daughter, became a champion horsewoman and has won almost as many prizes as an Olympic medallist. She and her husband are raising two beautiful daughters on their isolated farm in the Waihoki Valley.

For our three children the high point on their vacations in New Zealand was the picturesque mountainous farm on Mt. Adams. For them it was like Makara, a childhood Shangri-La. It was filled with deer, wild pigs, native pigeons and surprises and an exquisite glade of native bush. First acquired over 35 years ago by Brian and Geoffrey Mt. Adams today is owned and run by three of Geoffrey's sons.

Brother Patrick and his wife Liz brought up three sturdy boys on their Glendryneoch sheep farm. Over the years Liz's garden surrounding the homestead became a noted beauty spot in the pastureland an hour's drive from Martinborough.

Our first tragic losses among us siblings were our two sisters. First, Stellamaris in 1986. In an obituary published in the Wellington *Evening Post* it was noted: "Sister Stellamaris Diederich, of the Sisters of Mercy, Wellington, who died recently in Melbourne [Australia] was the daughter of Bernard and the late Stella Diederich of 75 Oxford Street, Martinborough."

The obituary continued:"Sister Stellamaris received her primary and secondary schooling at St. Mary's College. She entered the Sisters of Mercy, Wellington, in April 1946 and was professed in January 1949.

"That year she taught at St. Joseph's Primary School, Upper Hutt. In 1950 she went to the Mater Hospital, Auckland, to do general nursing training, which she completed at the end of 1953. This was followed up by maternity and midwifery training, and in the middle of 1955 she went to Mercy Hospital, Palmerston North, for a further four years. In 1960 she returned to St. Mary's College to teach, and remained on the staff until November 1983, when ill health forced her to resign.

"She was a very talented woman. Besides her qualifications as a nurse, she gained a B.A. from Victoria University and part of a Diploma in Fine Arts. She was a gifted artist and taught art with a great degree of success to the many pupils who passed through her hands at St. Mary's. She was a former prizewinner in the Kelliher Art Exhibition and her students won many art competitions under her tuition.

"To the underprivileged, the delinquent and the troubled she showed great compassion. For many years she visited the women's prison outside Wellington, and followed up its inmates when they were released, visiting and encouraging them. Many of her students experienced her concern for them and she was a confidante of many. She also had a special affinity for the sick. May she rest in peace."

A decade later, in 1996, Quita, who became a professional nurse and served in Australia also died of cancer. Shortly before her death she and her husband, along with their friends from her adopted Melbourne, walked in South America along trails in the high Andean mountain range. For Quita and her husband Bill, a cardiologist, walking was both a physical and spiritual exercise. Repeatedly they had walked along the "roof of the world" as she referred to hiking in Nepal.

Also as Quita lay dying she quietly made all the necessary arrangements for the future, which she would no longer enjoy. Surrounded by the deep love of her husband, three daughters, three sons, two of their wives and two grandchildren, it did seem at times that the power of their love might help her beat the cancer.

At her funeral I recalled in my eulogy our wonderful times together as children at Makara. "In my profession," I concluded, "I have seen many deaths, but Quita's is the most dignified I have ever witnessed." Which was true.

As literally hundreds of her friends and family filed out of that Melbourne church after the service one of her Australian friends approached me. Apologetically he asked me what my profession was to have witnessed so many deaths. A doctor like Quita's Bill? he asked. "No," I answered. "I'm a foreign correspondent who has covered too many wars and disasters and seen far too much human misery."

REFLECTIONS

In the year 2001 I had returned once again for a *Pamir* reunion and arriving two weeks early I decided it was time to see more of my homeland. The day we took the auto ferry from Wellington to Picton the sun shone. It continued to shine during our tour of New Zealand's South Island. This is important meteorological news to anyone familiar with the notorious fickle weather in the South Island especially on the West Coast our destination. "Take clothes for four seasons," I was warned time and again. "You can experience them all in one day." That late February trip was a glorious Indian—or more appropriately, Maori—summer.

In a world of shrinking forests, global warming, and urban sprawl, the South Island of New Zealand stands out as a monument to intelligent environmental management. My faith in my native land, which is endowed with such natural beauty, was restored.

Over the years I had returned home to New Zealand. Whether with my family on home leave from *Time* Magazine or to reunions with shipmates from those days when, at ages 16 or 17, we shared the unique experience of sailing the wide Pacific in the majestic four-masted barque *Pamir*, those visits were always trips back to the past, filled with nostalgia.

Some how it was only on this last trip, with longtime friend and author Ian Cross, his wife Tui and son Michael, that I discovered the New Zealand of today. And it was a fabulous awakening. The North Island had always been my destination and so with the eyes of a virtual newcomer I marveled at the wonders of the natureland that is the South Island. Scenic highways wound through pristine forests often dominated by Mount Cook, the "cloud

piercer," as the Maori's called the highest of the snow-capped Southern peaks, while large families of seals lazed on the sunny seashore.

Ian Cross later provided me with some facts, among them:
nearly 30 per cent of New Zealand, most of it covered by a mantle
of trees and bush, is protected by law as reserves and national
parks!

Enjoying the bountiful seafood fresh from the Tasman Sea at
the Southern Hotel in Hokitika, it was also heartwarming to learn
that conservation and protective laws also cover New Zealand's
coastlines, its fisheries and recreational areas. With ownership rights
extending a hundred miles out to sea from its lengthy coast lines—
including the Chatham Islands—New Zealand has territorial control over a significant part of the South Pacific and, it carefully
manages this, it may help sustain fishing stocks in perpetuity.

Gone was the claustrophobia that had tugged me away from
my small twin-island native country so long ago. New Zealand
has changed. No nation is perfect and New Zealand has its share
of unresolved problems, many paralleling those of the rest of the
world e.g., race; health and education services; a loss of talented
people overseas; foreign ownership and control of important bank-
ing and financial service owing to globalization.

The Maoris, who sailed in canoes to a land cloaked in clouds
more than a thousand years ago, christened it Aotearoa—"Land of
the long white cloud." Abel Tasman, a Dutch explorer visited in
1642 and in honor of his country named the new land New
Zealand.

Now the Maoris seek to have the country's name changed back
to Aotearoa. They cite the Treaty of Waitangi the founding document that was signed by the British colonizers and the Maori chiefs
in 1840, when the country became a colony of Queen Victoria.
The treaty is bound to protect indigenous culture and language.
Today both Maori and English are recognized as the country's
official languages.

Moreover with the communications highway running from
pole to pole fads good and bad are passed on throughout the world.
The warts of Western popular culture are too often shared. No

island remains an island in today's world. And this is true of New Zealand.

Nevertheless, New Zealanders will go to great lengths to save their own culture. It is perhaps best symbolized by the kiwi, a small, wingless, worm-pecking bird that hugs the forest floor. The kiwi and several other birds found in New Zealand are wingless because they had no natural predators until the immigrants arrived from the Northern Hemisphere. Today; New Zealanders proudly refer to themselves as "Kiwis."

As author Katherine Mansfield, who grew up near our family's Makara home, wrote in her journal:

"It's only by being true to life that I can be true to art. And to be true to life is to be good, genuine, simple and honest." It is an apt description of growing up in Makara.

G